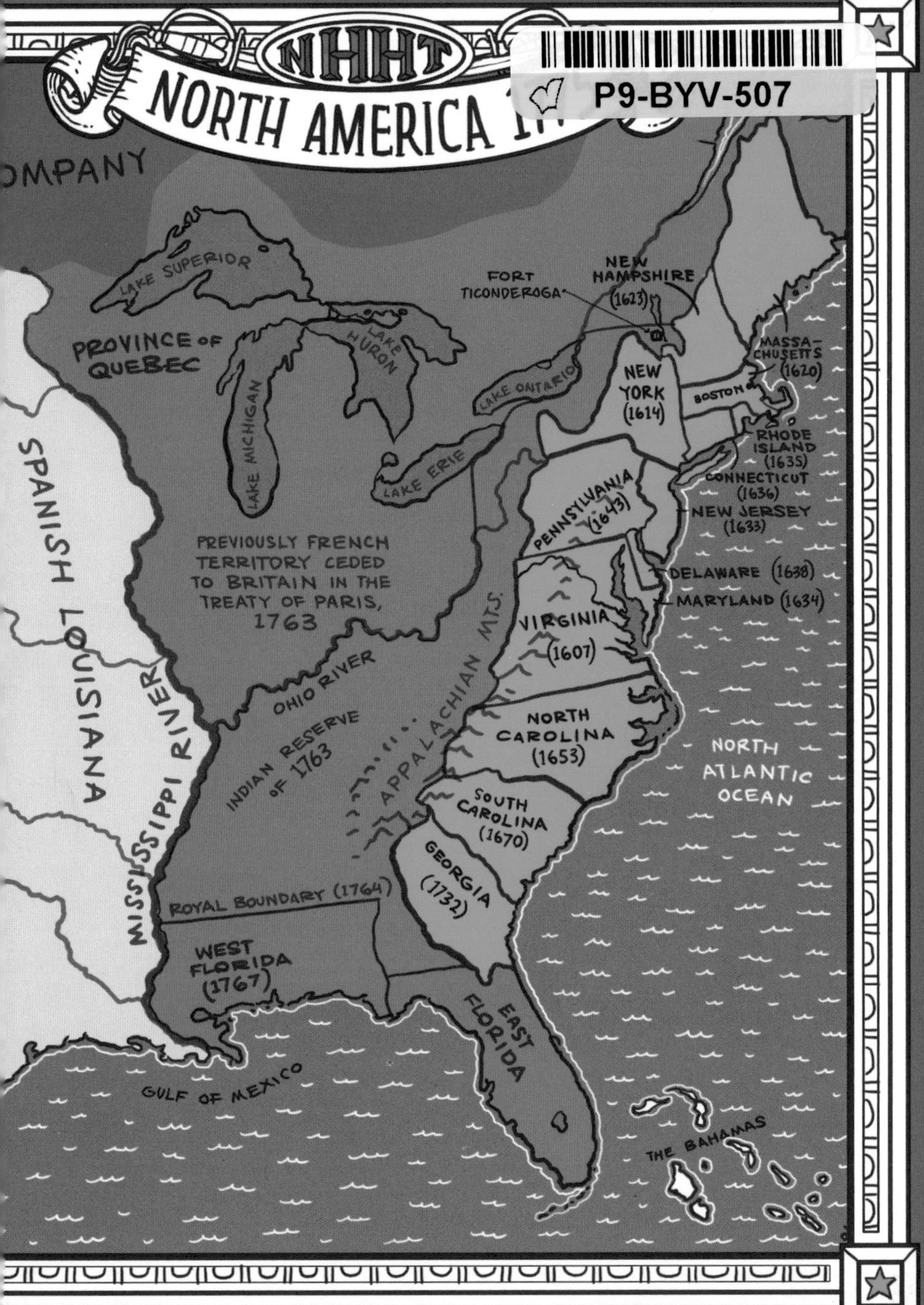

NHHT
NORTH AMERICA
OMPANY
LAKE SUPERIOR
PROVINCE OF QUEBEC
LAKE HURON
LAKE MICHIGAN
LAKE ONTARIO
LAKE ERIE
FORT TICONDEROGA
NEW HAMPSHIRE (1623)
MASSA-CHUSETTS (1620)
NEW YORK (1614)
BOSTON
RHODE ISLAND (1635)
CONNECTICUT (1636)
NEW JERSEY (1633)
PENNSYLVANIA (1643)
DELAWARE (1638)
MARYLAND (1634)
VIRGINIA (1607)
NORTH CAROLINA (1653)
SOUTH CAROLINA (1670)
GEORGIA (1732)
SPANISH LOUISIANA
PREVIOUSLY FRENCH TERRITORY CEDED TO BRITAIN IN THE TREATY OF PARIS, 1763
OHIO RIVER
APPALACHIAN MTS.
INDIAN RESERVE OF 1763
MISSISSIPPI RIVER
ROYAL BOUNDARY (1764)
WEST FLORIDA (1767)
EAST FLORIDA
NORTH ATLANTIC OCEAN
GULF OF MEXICO
THE BAHAMAS

NATHAN · HALE'S · HAZARDOUS · TALES

NHHT

THE HANGMAN

THE PROVOST

One Dead Spy

THE LIFE, TIMES, AND LAST WORDS OF NATHAN HALE, AMERICA'S MOST FAMOUS SPY

AMULET BOOKS, NEW YORK

LIBRARY OF CONGRESS CONTROL NUMBER 2012947189
ISBN 978-1-4197-0396-6

TEXT AND ILLUSTRATIONS COPYRIGHT © 2012 NATHAN HALE
BOOK DESIGN BY NATHAN HALE AND CHAD W. BECKERMAN

PRINTED AND BOUND IN CHINA
25 24 23 22

AMULET BOOKS ARE AVAILABLE AT SPECIAL DISCOUNTS WHEN
PURCHASED IN QUANTITY FOR PREMIUMS AND PROMOTIONS
AS WELL AS FUNDRAISING OR EDUCATIONAL USE. SPECIAL
EDITIONS CAN ALSO BE CREATED TO SPECIFICATION. FOR
DETAILS, CONTACT SPECIALSALES@ABRAMSBOOKS.COM OR
THE ADDRESS BELOW.

ABRAMS The Art of Books
195 Broadway, New York, NY 10007
abramsbooks.com

FOR MINDY

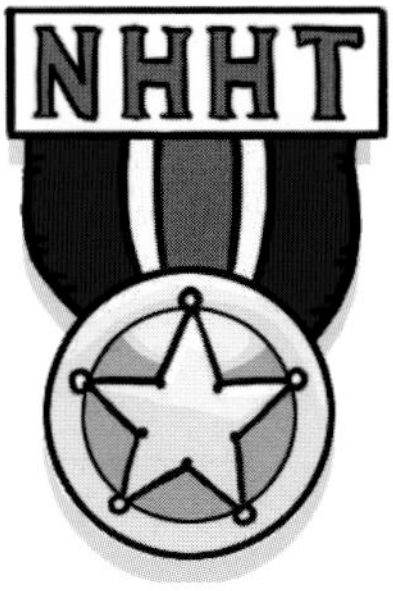
NHHT

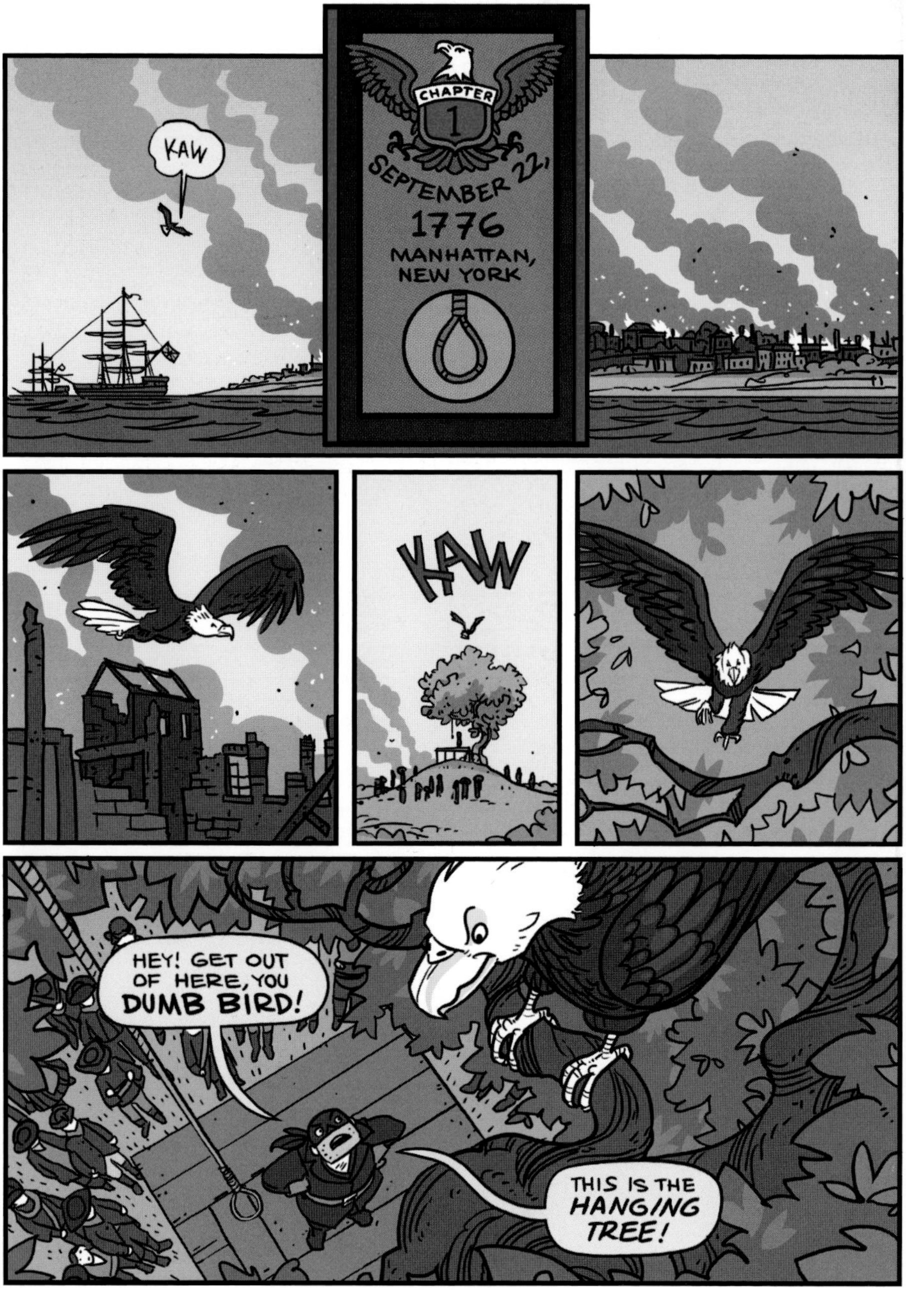
CHAPTER
1
SEPTEMBER 22,
1776
MANHATTAN, NEW YORK
KAW
KAW
HEY! GET OUT OF HERE, YOU DUMB BIRD!
THIS IS THE HANGING TREE!

WELCOME, ONE AND ALL! I AM THE **HANGMAN**. I AM HERE TO *HANG* THE *MAN!*

WHO ARE YOU HANGING TODAY?

IS IT THE PERSON WHO STARTED THE BIG FIRE?

UM, DON'T THINK SO.

WE WANT THE **FIRE STARTER!**

HANG THE ARSONIST!

HALF *THE CITY'S* BURNED DOWN!

HANG 'IM!

LET ME SEE, WE DON'T HAVE ANY ARSONISTS...

WE HAVE... ...HMMM...

A SPY.

KAW

YOU'RE HANGIN' A LOUSY SPY?

SPIES ARE LOWLIFES-- GOOD FOR NOTHIN'!

TELL US WHEN YOU CATCH THE ARSONIST. *THAT* WILL BE A HANGIN' WORTH SEEIN'.

HEY! COME BACK! DON'T YOU WANT TO SEE ME HANG THIS *SPY*?

YOU CAN PRETEND HE STARTED THE FIRE!

7

MAKE WAY FOR THE PRISONER!

MAKE WAY FOR THE SPY!

I HAVE A SPY HERE, MR. HANGMAN. WHAT DO WE DO WITH SPIES?

WE HANG SPIES!

THAT IS CORRECT! SPYING AGAINST YOUR KING AND COUNTRY IS PUNISHABLE BY DEATH!

I HAVE ORDERS TO... UM...

HUH? WHERE ARE THE BLASTED HANGING ORDERS?

WE CAN'T HANG HIM WITHOUT THE ORDERS. I MUST HAVE LEFT THEM SOMEWHERE...

...BE RIGHT BACK.

THIS IS AWKWARD.

DO YOU...UH, WANT TO PRACTICE YOUR, UM, **LAST WORDS** MR...?

HALE, *NATHAN HALE*.

I HAVEN'T THOUGHT ABOUT MY LAST WORDS.

I'VE HEARD SOME REAL **DOOZIES** IN MY TIME. I CAN GIVE YOU SOME IDEAS.

BUT... THEN THEY WOULDN'T BE **MY** LAST WORDS.

HOW ABOUT... "*I AM GOING TO TAKE MY LAST VOYAGE...*" SOMETHING REAL POETIC- LIKE?

OR SOMETHING ANGRY, LIKE "DOWN WITH ALL OF YOU!"

WELL...

REGRETS! DO YOU HAVE ANY REGRETS?

I REGRET THAT I ONLY HAVE ONE LIFE.

HA HA! GOOD ONE! IF YOU HAD AN EXTRA LIFE YOU COULD BE HANGED, THEN JUST WALK AWAY.

ANYTHING ELSE?

NOT REALLY.

NO REGRETS?

NO. I SPIED FOR MY COUNTRY AND I'D DO IT AGAIN.

AH! **PATRIOTIC** STUFF! THAT'S GOOD! HOW ABOUT, "GIVE ME LIBERTY OR GIVE ME -- WHAT WAS IT?-- A **SANDWICH!**"

NO, NO. IT WAS, "GIVE ME LIBERTY OR GIVE ME *DEATH*."

PATRICK HENRY SAID THAT LAST YEAR.

NOW **THOSE** ARE SOME GREAT LAST WORDS!

THOSE WEREN'T HIS LAST WORDS. HE SAID THEM IN A SPEECH. PATRICK HENRY IS THE GOVERNOR OF VIRGINIA.

"GIVE ME LIBERTY OR GIVE ME AN **EXTRA LIFE** SO I CAN DIE FOR MY COUNTRY **TWO TIMES.**" HOW'S THAT?

HMM. THAT'S NOT GREAT...

"GIVE ME A **SANDWICH** OR GIVE ME DEATH!"

YOU **REALLY** WANT A SANDWICH.

YES, I DO.

I REGRET THAT I DO NOT HAVE A SANDWICH TO GIVE YOU.

THAT'S ALL RIGHT, I HAVE A SANDWICH WAITING FOR ME AT HOME.

YOU SEEM LIKE A NICE FELLOW. I REGRET THAT I DO NOT HAVE AN **EXTRA LIFE** TO GIVE YOU.

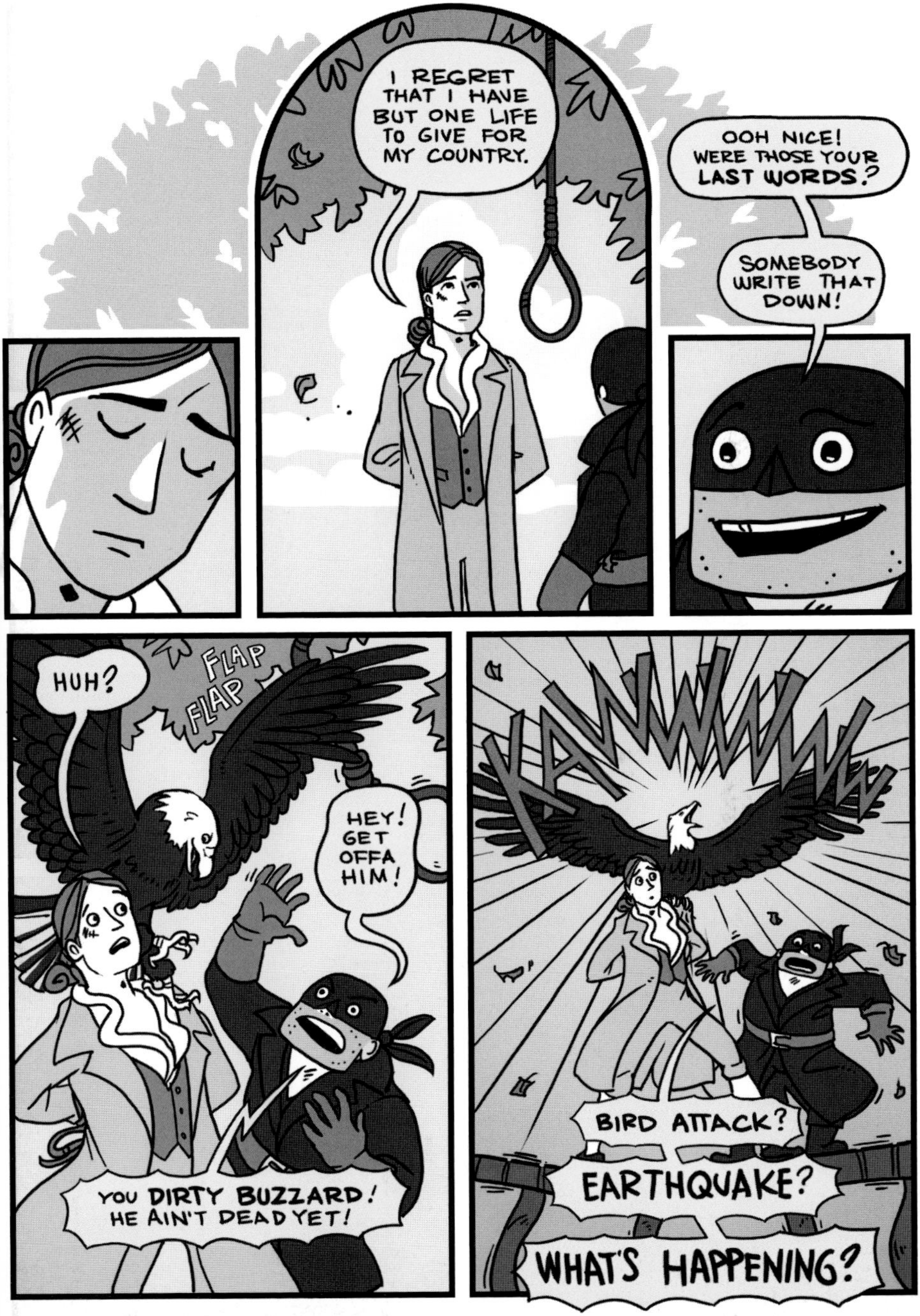
I REGRET THAT I HAVE BUT ONE LIFE TO GIVE FOR MY COUNTRY.
OOH NICE! WERE THOSE YOUR LAST WORDS?
SOMEBODY WRITE THAT DOWN!
HUH?
FLAP FLAP
HEY! GET OFFA HIM!
YOU DIRTY BUZZARD! HE AIN'T DEAD YET!
KAWWWWW
BIRD ATTACK?
EARTHQUAKE?
WHAT'S HAPPENING?

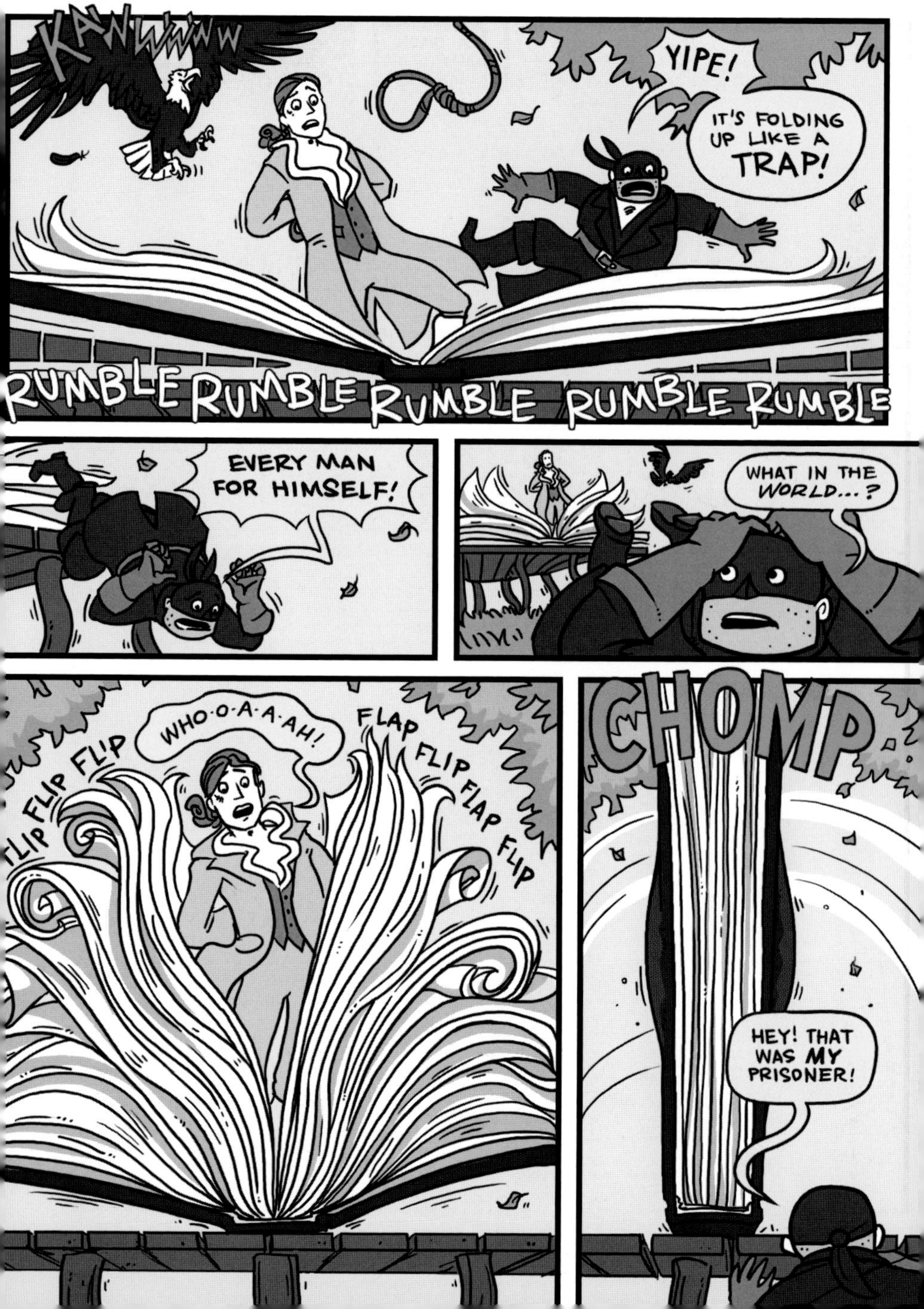
KA'NWWWW
YIPE!
IT'S FOLDING UP LIKE A TRAP!
RUMBLE RUMBLE RUMBLE RUMBLE RUMBLE
EVERY MAN FOR HIMSELF!
WHAT IN THE WORLD...?
WHO-O-A-A-AH!
FLIP FLIP FLIP
FLAP FLIP FLAP FLIP
CHOMP
HEY! THAT WAS MY PRISONER!

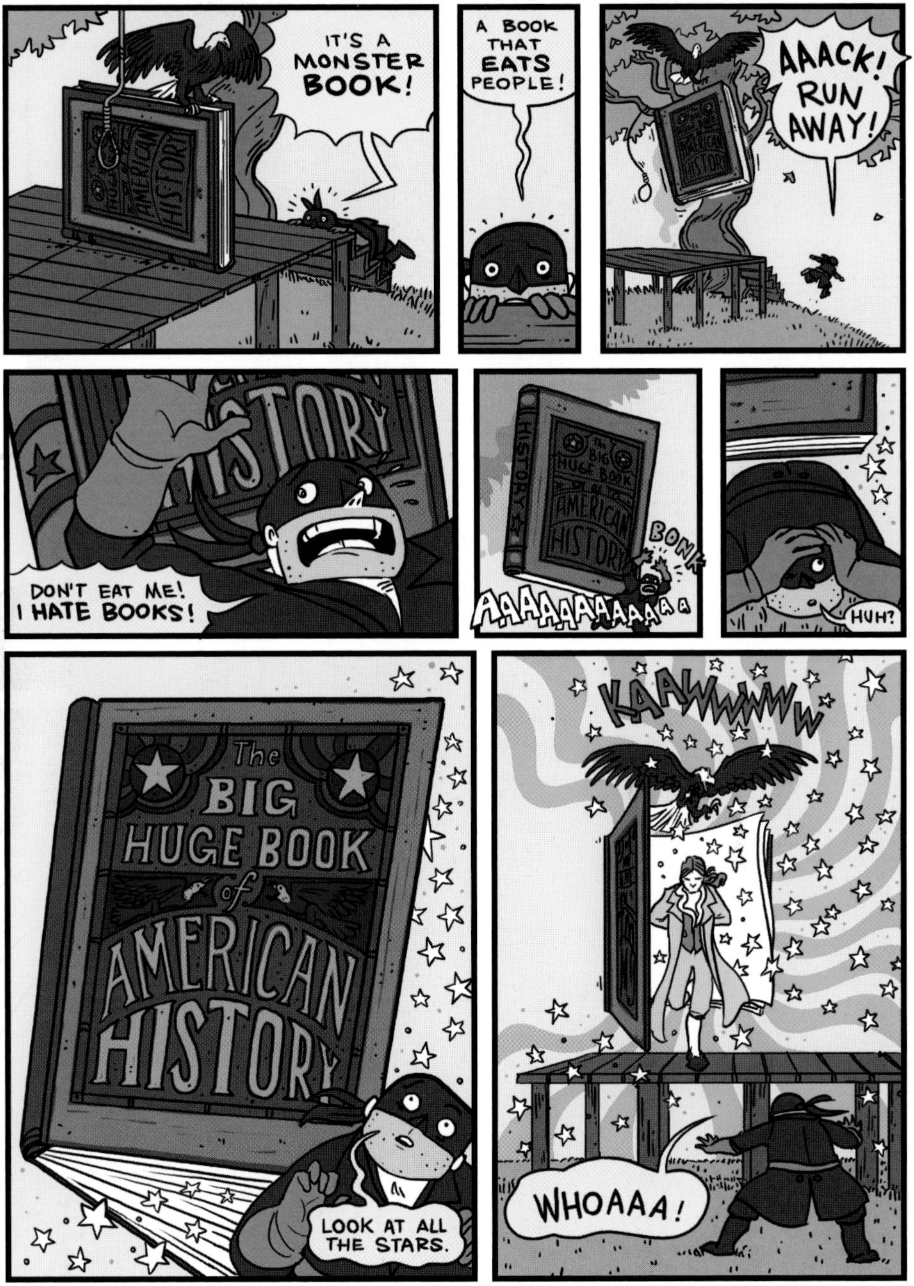
IT'S A MONSTER BOOK!
A BOOK THAT EATS PEOPLE!
AAACK! RUN AWAY!
DON'T EAT ME! I HATE BOOKS!
HISTORY
The BIG HUGE BOOK of AMERICAN HISTORY
BONK
AAAAAAAAAAAA
HUH?
The BIG HUGE BOOK of AMERICAN HISTORY
LOOK AT ALL THE STARS.
KAAWWWWW
WHOAAA!

YOU'RE BACK!?

HELLO.

"HELLO," he says. *HELLO?* WHAT IN BLUE BLAZES *JUST HAPPENED!??*

THIS IS "THE BIG HUGE BOOK OF AMERICAN HISTORY."

I JUST MADE HISTORY.

YOU *WHAT?*

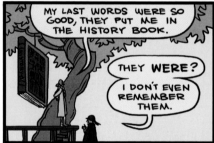

MY LAST WORDS WERE SO GOOD, THEY PUT ME IN THE HISTORY BOOK.

THEY *WERE?*

I DON'T EVEN REMEMBER THEM.

"I REGRET THAT I HAVE BUT ONE LIFE TO GIVE FOR MY COUNTRY."

SO DO I, BUT I STILL CAN'T REMEMBER WHAT YOUR LAST WORDS WERE.

WHAT'S INSIDE THAT GIANT BOOK?

THE HISTORY OF THIS COUNTRY. I SAW IT *ALL* --HUNDREDS OF YEARS INTO THE FUTURE.

HOW COULD YOU SEE THE *FUTURE* IN A *HISTORY* BOOK?

IT DOESN'T MAKE ANY SENSE.

A GIANT BOOK JUST SWALLOWED ME WHOLE. DOES *THAT* MAKE ANY SENSE?

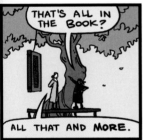

WHAT DID YOU **SEE** IN THE FUTURE?

I SAW THE BIRTH OF THIS NATION.

I SAW **WARS**, HEROES, AND VILLAINS...

EXPLORERS AND **INVENTORS**...

IRON SHIPS, **FLYING SHIPS**...

MILLIONS OF LIVES, MILLIONS OF **STORIES!**

THAT'S ALL IN THE BOOK?

ALL THAT AND **MORE**.

PROVE IT! IF YOU CAN SEE THE FUTURE, WHAT AM I GOING TO HAVE FOR LUNCH TODAY?

A SANDWICH?

BY JOVE! YOU **DID** SEE THE FUTURE!

KAWWWW

UH-OH! NOW WHAT?

IT'S GOING WIGGLY!

KAW

POOF

POOF? THERE IT GOES.

I FOUND THE HANGING ORDERS.

DID I MISS ANYTHING?

15

YOU ONLY MISSED THE **MOST AMAZING** THING I'VE EVER SEEN!

OH, REALLY? WHAT WAS THAT?

A **GIANT BOOK** CAME OUT OF NOWHERE AND **SWALLOWED** HIM WHOLE!

UH-HUH...

NOW HE CAN SEE THE **FUTURE!**

UH-HUH-- **WHAT?**

HE KNEW *EXACTLY* WHAT I WAS GOING TO HAVE FOR LUNCH TODAY!

A SANDWICH?

WHA--

DID THE BOOK EAT YOU TOO?

ENOUGH OF THIS NONSENSE. LET'S GET THIS HANGING OVER WITH.

WHERE'S OUR AUDIENCE?

THEY DON'T WANT TO SEE A SPY HANG. THEY WANT TO SEE THE **ARSONIST** HANG.

SO DO I. I HOPE THEY CATCH THE DEVIL SOON.

THEY NEVER CATCH THE ARSONIST.

HOW DO YOU KNOW?

I TOLD YOU! HE CAN **SEE THE FUTURE!**

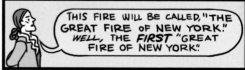

THIS FIRE WILL BE CALLED, "THE GREAT FIRE OF NEW YORK." WELL, THE *FIRST* "GREAT FIRE OF NEW YORK."

OH NO! THERE'S *ANOTHER* FIRE?

YES, BUT NOT UNTIL 1835.

1835? WHAT ARE YOU *TALKING* ABOUT?

THE FUTURE! HISTORY!

ENOUGH OF YOUR SILLY GAMES! THIS IS AN EXECUTION!

THERE IS NO PLACE FOR *HUMOR* ON THE GALLOWS.

WHAT ABOUT GALLOWS HUMOR?

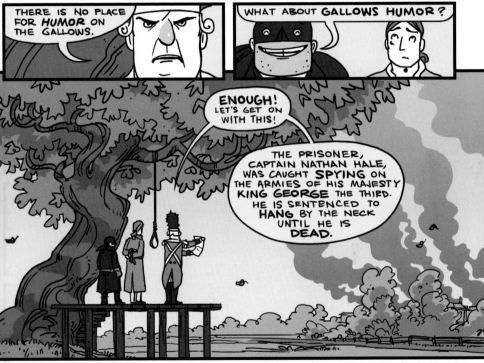

ENOUGH! LET'S GET ON WITH THIS!

THE PRISONER, CAPTAIN NATHAN HALE, WAS CAUGHT **SPYING** ON THE ARMIES OF HIS MAJESTY KING **GEORGE** THE THIRD. HE IS SENTENCED TO **HANG** BY THE NECK UNTIL HE IS **DEAD.**

DOES IT HAPPEN? DO YOU GET HANGED IN THE FUTURE?

YES, I DO.

AIN'T YOU SCARED?

YES, I'M SCARED. WOULDN'T YOU BE?

17

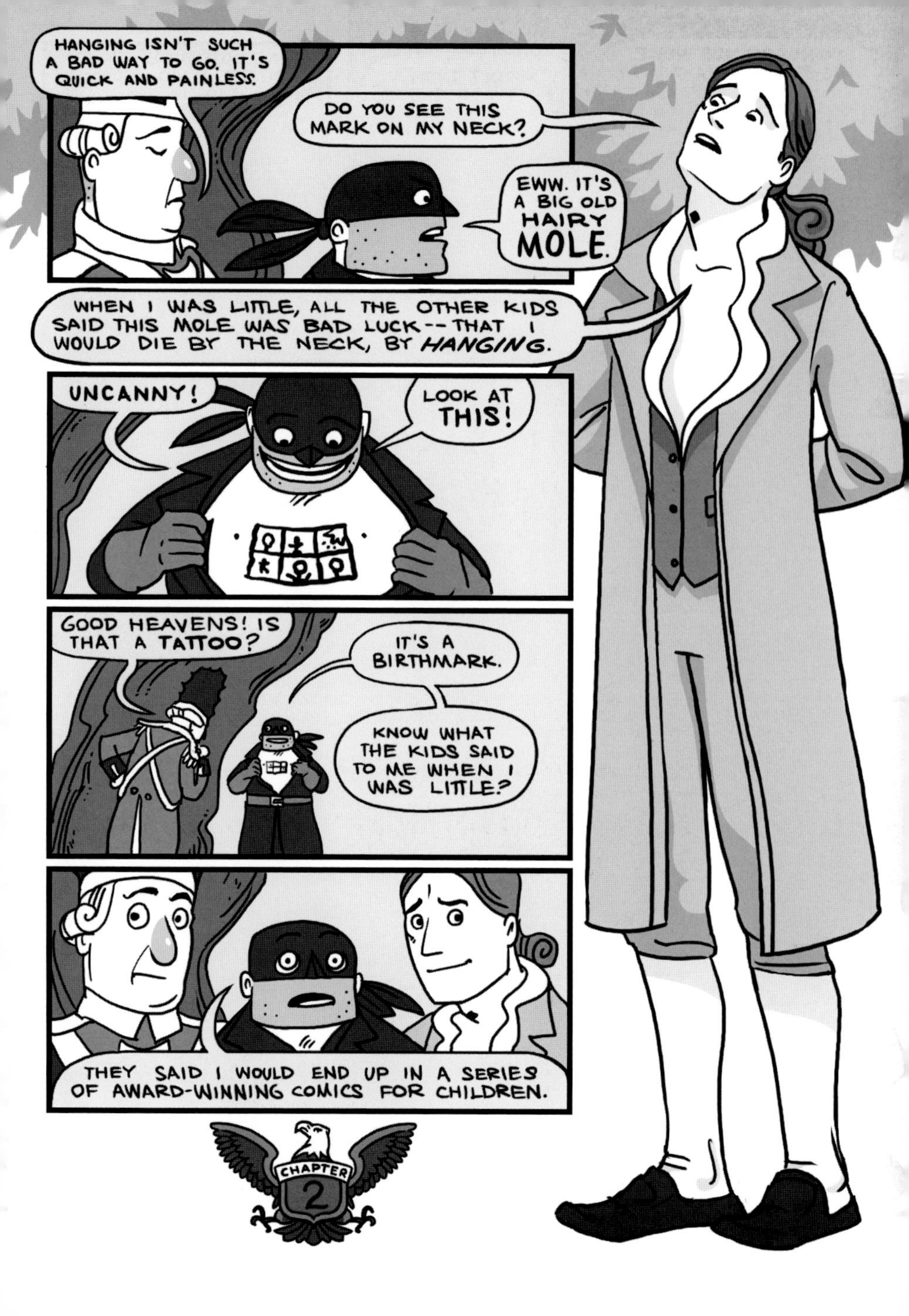
HANGING ISN'T SUCH A BAD WAY TO GO. IT'S QUICK AND PAINLESS.
DO YOU SEE THIS MARK ON MY NECK?
EWW. IT'S A BIG OLD HAIRY MOLE.
WHEN I WAS LITTLE, ALL THE OTHER KIDS SAID THIS MOLE WAS BAD LUCK -- THAT I WOULD DIE BY THE NECK, BY HANGING.
UNCANNY!
LOOK AT THIS!
GOOD HEAVENS! IS THAT A TATTOO?
IT'S A BIRTHMARK.
KNOW WHAT THE KIDS SAID TO ME WHEN I WAS LITTLE?
THEY SAID I WOULD END UP IN A SERIES OF AWARD-WINNING COMICS FOR CHILDREN.
CHAPTER
2

YOUR FRIENDS WERE RIGHT, YOU **WILL** DIE BY HANGING, AS ALL SPIES DO.

I WASN'T EVEN A VERY GOOD SPY. I WAS CAPTURED ON MY FIRST MISSION.

YOU WERE?

I WAS OUTSPIED BY AN **EXPERT.** I NOW KNOW WHAT I DID WRONG -- I'VE SEEN IT ALL.

IN THE BIG BOOK?

YUP.

OOH! TELL US THE STORY!

I'D LIKE TO HEAR IT MYSELF.

BUT NO MORE ABOUT THE SILLY GIANT BOOK!

MY STORY STARTS AT YALE.

HA-HA! HALE AT YALE.

I WENT TO YALE COLLEGE IN 1769. I WAS FOURTEEN.

IS THIS SOME KIND OF **SPY** TRICK?

A **MAGIC** FLOATING WINDOW!

THIS IS WHAT I SAW IN THE BIG BOOK.

THINK OF IT AS A WINDOW INTO HISTORY.

ARE YOU A **WIZARD?**

NO. I'M JUST A SPY WITH A STORY TO TELL.

A **DEAD** SPY.

OH BOY! LET'S GET THIS STORY ROLLING!

YALE WAS A VERY **LARGE** COLLEGE. THERE WERE NEARLY **100** STUDENTS.

WAS IT A **SPY** COLLEGE?

NO, BUT SOME OF US BECAME SPIES.

A HIVE OF TRAITORS!

I WAS THERE WITH MY BEST FRIEND **BEN TALLMADGE**.

WE WERE STUDYING TO BE TEACHERS.

WE WOKE UP EVERY MORNING AT FOUR FOR PRAYERS.

FOUR A.M.!?! HOW HORRIBLE

WE STUDIED GREEK,

ἦλθον, εἶδον, ἐνίκησα!

BORING.

WE STUDIED LATIN,

"DULCE ET DECORUM EST PRO PATRIA MORI."

BORING.

WE STUDIED PHILOSOPHY.

"THE LOVE OF DEMOCRACY IS THAT OF EQUALITY."

BORING!

WE PLAYED SPORTS.

WHAT SPORTS?

I WAS A VERY GOOD WRESTLER.

I BET I COULD WRESTLE YOU! LET'S **WRESTLE!**

YOU WILL DO **NO** SUCH THING!

AWW.

DID YOU DO **ANYTHING** FUN AT YALE?

WELL...THERE WAS THIS ONE TIME AT THE TAVERN...

AW YEAH!

20

READ 'EM AND WEEP, BOYS!

I LOST AGAIN!? THAT'S MY TWENTY-FIRST LOSING HAND!

HA-HA! YOU HAVE THE WORST LUCK OF ANYONE I KNOW.

WHAT? I'M LUCKY!

WHAT DO YOU THINK, BOYS, IS NATE LUCKY?

NO! NOT A BIT!

HE AIN'T LUCKY AT ALL!

THEY'RE RIGHT. YOU ARE NOT LUCKY.

I AM TOO LUCKY! ALL THE GIRLS IN TOWN LIKE ME!

THAT'S TRU-U-UE!

YES, BUT ARE YOU ENGAGED TO ONE OF THEM?

WELL... NO, BUT...

UNLUCKY! UNLUCKY!

I PROPOSE A LUCK TEST!

NOT IN MY TAVERN! TEST THAT UNLUCKY LAD OUTSIDE.

RIGHT THIS WAY!

LUCK TEST! LUCK TEST!

21

HERE IS YOUR LUCK TESTER.

A ROCK?

JUST THROW IT IN ANY DIRECTION.

WHY?

BECAUSE IT WILL LAND SOMEWHERE *UNLUCKY*.

HUH?

JUST THROW IT!

OKAY.

FWISH

LISTEN...

CRASH

OH NO! I BROKE A WINDOW?

THAT WAS A **SCHOOL** WINDOW.

THAT WAS THE HEADMASTER'S WINDOW!

YIPE!

I STILL DON'T BELIEVE IT.

THEN TRY AGAIN.

FLING

CRASH

THAT WAS THE SENIORS' DORMITORY.

ZIP

CRASH

CHAPEL.

CHUCK

CRASH

HEADMASTER'S OFFICE AGAIN.

WOW.

UH. THAT'S ENOUGH.

NO MORE ROCKS FOR YOU!

BUT—

UNLUCKY!

22

HERE IS THE BILL FOR YOUR ROCK-THROWING SPREE.

HEADMASTER'S OFFICE

I'M SORRY, SIR, I WAS TESTING MY LUCK.

THEN I'D SAY YOU HAVE HORRIBLE LUCK,

BUT A GOOD THROWING ARM.

EVERYONE AT YALE WAS TALKING ABOUT REVOLUTION.

AGAINST WHAT?

AGAINST THE CROWN—— ENGLAND! WE WANT TO BE OUR OWN COUNTRY.

WHAT DID YOU THINK THIS WAR WAS ABOUT?

WAIT, THERE'S A WAR GOING ON?

OF COURSE THERE'S A WAR GOING ON, YOU MELON-HEADED GOON!

DON'T YOU SEE THE ARMIES? THE FIRES? THE SPIES GETTING HANGED?!

JUST SEEMS LIKE BUSINESS AS USUAL.

BUSINESS AS USUAL?!

WE'RE IN THE MIDDLE OF A MAJOR WAR!

WITH WHO? THE FRENCH? THE INDIANS?

THE FRENCH AND INDIANS?

THE FRENCH AND INDIAN WAR ENDED THIRTEEN YEARS AGO! YOU NITWIT!

IT WAS? WHO WON?

WE DID, YOU NUMBSKULL!

WE DROVE THE FRENCH OUT!

WE DID?

HUH. YOU LEARN SOMETHING NEW EVERY DAY.

CHAPTER 3

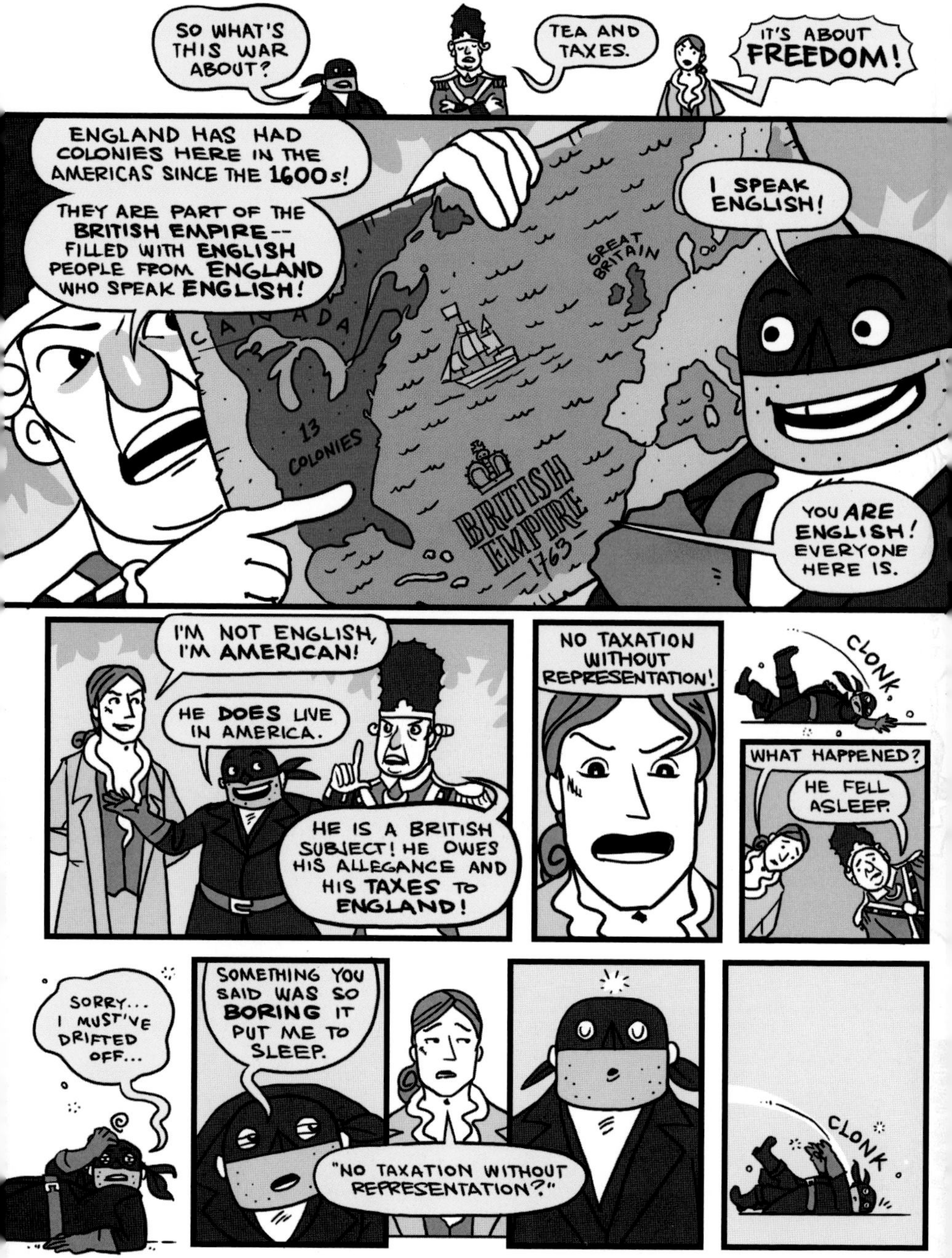

SO WHAT'S THIS WAR ABOUT?
TEA AND TAXES.
IT'S ABOUT FREEDOM!
ENGLAND HAS HAD COLONIES HERE IN THE AMERICAS SINCE THE 1600s!
THEY ARE PART OF THE BRITISH EMPIRE-- FILLED WITH ENGLISH PEOPLE FROM ENGLAND WHO SPEAK ENGLISH!
CANADA
13 COLONIES
GREAT BRITAIN
BRITISH EMPIRE 1763
I SPEAK ENGLISH!
YOU ARE ENGLISH! EVERYONE HERE IS.
I'M NOT ENGLISH, I'M AMERICAN!
HE DOES LIVE IN AMERICA.
HE IS A BRITISH SUBJECT! HE OWES HIS ALLEGANCE AND HIS TAXES TO ENGLAND!
NO TAXATION WITHOUT REPRESENTATION!
CLONK
WHAT HAPPENED?
HE FELL ASLEEP.
SORRY... I MUST'VE DRIFTED OFF...
SOMETHING YOU SAID WAS SO BORING IT PUT ME TO SLEEP.
"NO TAXATION WITHOUT REPRESENTATION?"
CLONK

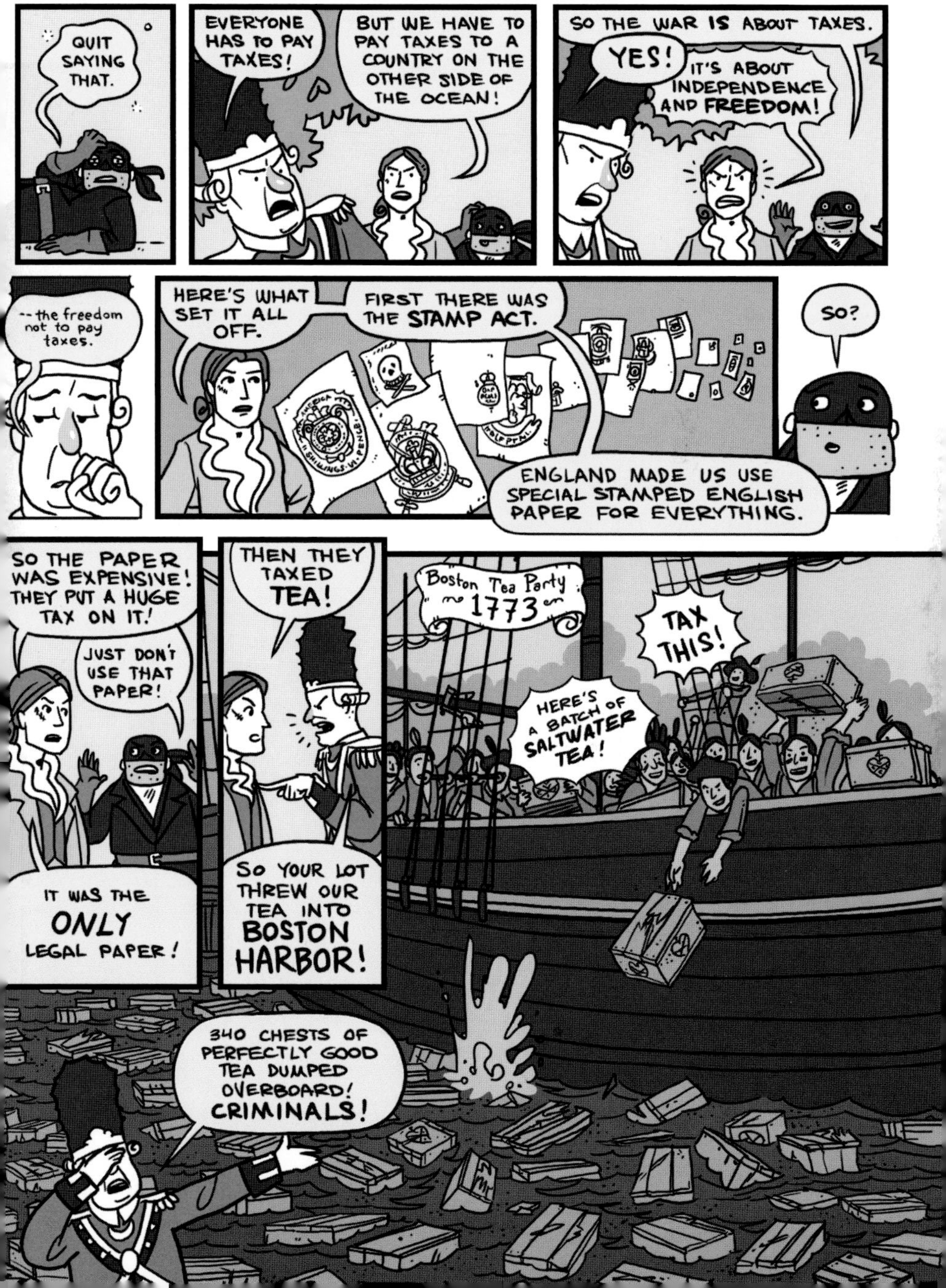

QUIT SAYING THAT.
EVERYONE HAS TO PAY TAXES!
BUT WE HAVE TO PAY TAXES TO A COUNTRY ON THE OTHER SIDE OF THE OCEAN!
SO THE WAR IS ABOUT TAXES.
YES!
IT'S ABOUT INDEPENDENCE AND FREEDOM!
--the freedom not to pay taxes.
HERE'S WHAT SET IT ALL OFF.
FIRST THERE WAS THE STAMP ACT.
SO?
ENGLAND MADE US USE SPECIAL STAMPED ENGLISH PAPER FOR EVERYTHING.
SO THE PAPER WAS EXPENSIVE! THEY PUT A HUGE TAX ON IT!
JUST DON'T USE THAT PAPER!
IT WAS THE ONLY LEGAL PAPER!
THEN THEY TAXED TEA!
SO YOUR LOT THREW OUR TEA INTO BOSTON HARBOR!
Boston Tea Party
1773
TAX THIS!
HERE'S A BATCH OF SALTWATER TEA!
340 CHESTS OF PERFECTLY GOOD TEA DUMPED OVERBOARD! CRIMINALS!

THEN **YOU** CLOSED THE PORT OF BOSTON!

A **NASTY** THING TO DO AFTER WHAT YOU **BRITISH** DID IN 1770!

WHAT HAPPENED IN 1770?

THE **BOSTON** MASSACRE!

MASSACRE? THE PEOPLE OF BOSTON STARTED IT!

THEY THREW ROCKS AT BRITISH TROOPS!

AND THE BRITISH FOUGHT BACK WITH **GUNS!**

The Boston Massacre 1770

THIS ISN'T HOW IT HAPPENED! WHO DREW THIS?

ROCKS VS. GUNS? THAT'S NOT FAIR!

DRAWN BY PAUL REVERE

FIVE UNARMED PEOPLE WERE KILLED!

THEY SHOULDN'T HAVE THROWN ROCKS AT ARMED SOLDIERS!!

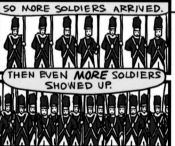

SO MORE SOLDIERS ARRIVED.

THEN EVEN **MORE** SOLDIERS SHOWED UP.

AND YOU STARTED WHINING ABOUT BEING YOUR OWN COUNTRY.

OOOH! WE'RE **SO** INDEPENDENT.'

OKAY. LET ME GET THIS STRAIGHT;

YOU DON'T LIKE STAMPED PAPER,

YOU THREW TEA IN THE OCEAN,

YEAH, THAT'S ABOUT IT.

YOU WANT AMERICA TO BE ITS OWN COUNTRY...

YOU GOT ROWDY WITH SOLDIERS IN BOSTON,

...BUT ENGLAND WANTS TO KEEP IT, AND SENT OVER A BUNCH OF REDCOATS.

SO NOW IT'S A **WAR.**

IS THAT IT?

IN A NUTSHELL

BUT THERE'S NO ARMY HERE TO FIGHT THE REDCOATS.

HA! YOU'VE GOT THAT RIGHT.

WE'VE GOT AN ARMY!

YOU DO?

WHAT COLOR IS YOUR UNIFORM? THE ONLY ARMY I EVER SEE WEARS RED.

THEY DON'T *HAVE* UNIFORMS! THEY AREN'T A PROPER ARMY AT ALL. THEY'RE JUST A BUNCH OF *FARMERS.*

THEIR UNIFORM IS DIRTY CLOTHES.

DIRTY CLOTHES, EH?

I HOPE NOBODY MISTAKES ME FOR ONE OF THEM.

WE ARE LED BY GENERAL GEORGE WASHINGTON.

GEORGE WASHA--WHO?

GEORGE WASHINGTON. HE'S FROM VIRGINIA. HE LOOKS LIKE THIS.

WOW! NOW THAT'S A UNIFORM!

MEH. THIS IS MY GEORGE. KING GEORGE.

DOUBLE WOW!

GEORGE VS. GEORGE.

THEY SORT OF LOOK THE SAME.

BY GEORGE! THEY *DO* LOOK THE SAME!

HOW AM I SUPPOSED TO TELL THEM APART?

DON'T WORRY, KING GEORGE NEVER COMES TO AMERICA.

WHAT ABOUT GEORGE WASHY-TOES?

OH, WE SEE A *LOT* OF HIM.

HAVE THERE BEEN ANY GOOD BATTLES IN THIS WAR?

CHAPTER 4

OF COURSE THERE HAVE BEEN BATTLES! EVEN THOUGH THE AMERICAN ARMY IS JUST A BUNCH OF RAGTAG BUMPKINS!

I'M A **CAPTAIN** IN THE AMERICAN ARMY. WE CALL OURSELVES THE **CONTINENTAL ARMY**.

HAVE **YOU** SEEN ANY BATTLES?

I'VE SEEN THEM **ALL**-- IN THE BIG HISTORY BOOK.

IN *PERSON!* WERE YOU IN ANY BATTLES.

MY STORY IS A **SPY'S** STORY. BUT THERE ARE BATTLES IN IT.

SO GET ON WITH IT!

AFTER YALE, I GOT MY FIRST JOB AS A TEACHER.

THIS ISN'T A SPY **OR** BATTLE STORY! NOTHING EXCITING IS HAPPENING!

DON'T YOU THINK THE EDUCATION OF YOUNG PEOPLE IS EXCITING?

NOT. AT. ALL.

I WAS TEACHING WHEN I HEARD ABOUT THE FIRST BATTLES OF THE WAR.

SIR! THE BRITISH ARE ATTACKING AT LEXINGTON AND CONCORD!

I SAID:

LET US MARCH IMMEDIATELY AND NEVER LAY DOWN ARMS UNTIL WE OBTAIN OUR INDEPENDENCE!

HEY. THOSE ARE GOOD LAST WORDS TOO!

I SAID GOOD-BYE TO MY STUDENTS AND JOINED THE CONNECTICUT MILITIA.

WOO HOO! SCHOOL'S OUT!

I WAS MADE A LIEUTENANT IN THE CONNECTICUT 7TH REGIMENT.

ALMOST EVERYONE FROM YALE WAS GOING INTO THE ARMY.

BUT NOT MY FRIEND BEN TALLMADGE.

Dear Ben, I am a lieutenant! —Nate

Dear Nate, I am going to stay a Teacher. —Ben

I WANTED TO MARCH STRAIGHT TO WASHINGTON'S CAMP. BUT WE HAD TO WAIT FOR A FEW MONTHS.

WHY?

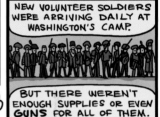

NEW VOLUNTEER SOLDIERS WERE ARRIVING DAILY AT WASHINGTON'S CAMP.

BUT THERE WEREN'T ENOUGH SUPPLIES OR EVEN GUNS FOR ALL OF THEM.

SNORT AN ARMY WITH NO GUNS! WHAT A JOKE!

WE SPENT ALL OF OUR TIME PRACTICING AND RECRUITING MORE VOLUNTEERS.

BY THE TIME WE MOVED TO THE FRONT I HAD BEEN MADE A CAPTAIN.

WE MARCHED FOR BOSTON.

BOSTON

SOME TOWNS WE MARCHED THROUGH CHEERED FOR US,

...AND SOME DIDN'T.

SOME TOWNS ARE STILL LOYAL TO THE CROWN!

WE WERE STATIONED OUTSIDE OF BOSTON, IN A TOWN CALLED **ROXBURY**.

SERGEANT HEMPSTEAD, WE'RE NOT AT YALE ANYMORE.

THERE MUST BE 10,000 SOLDIERS CAMPED HERE!

5,000 IS MORE ACCURATE.

HELLO, SOLDIER.

I'M HENRY KNOX.

I'M CAPTAIN HALE AND THIS IS SERGEANT HEMPSTEAD.

I RAN A BOOKSTORE IN BOSTON -- NOW I CAN'T GET BACK IN!

THOSE FILTHY **LOBSTERBACKS** HAVE TAKEN OVER THE WHOLE CITY.

WHAT'S A LOBSTERBACK? SOME KINDA **MONSTER**?

A BRITISH SOLDIER, RED-BACKED, LIKE A LOBSTER.

YOU'RE JUST JEALOUS OF OUR UNIFORMS.

I HAVE A PLAN TO WIN BACK BOSTON. I'M OFF TO TELL GENERAL WASHINGTON.

WHAT SORTA PLAN?

WAIT AND SEE, CAP'N HALE!

WAIT AND SEE!

WHAT AN ODD FELLOW.

ANY IDEA WHERE OUR REGIMENT IS IN THIS MESSY CAMP?

THIS IS WHAT ALL ARMY CAMPS ARE LIKE.

NOT TRUE!

SHOW A BRITISH CAMP!

TAKE A GOOD LOOK! **THAT'S** HOW PROFESSIONALS MAKE CAMP.

THE TWO CAMPS WERE ACTUALLY VERY CLOSE TO EACH OTHER.

THE BRITISH

BOSTON

BOSTON NECK

US

ROXBURY

KEEP YOUR HEADS DOWN, BOYS. THE REDCOATS ARE RIGHT NEXT DOOR!

THEY KEEP US ON OUR TOES WITH CANNON FIRE.

BUT WE SEND IT RIGHT BACK!

BOOM

GET DOWN!

YIKES!

HMMM. SOUNDS LIKE A 11-POUNDER, FIRING HOLLOW SHOT...

BOOM

ISN'T THIS GREAT?

HUH?

I LOVE GUNS AND ARTILLERY!

BOOM

I THOUGHT YOU WERE A BOOK-SELLER.

I WAS. I SPENT ALL DAY READING BOOKS ABOUT GUNS AND ARTILLERY!

AAAGH!

WHAT HAPPENED TO YOUR HAND!?!

AAAAAAGH!

AAAAAGH!

HA-HA-HA!

SORRY. THAT WAS MEAN. I LOST THESE FINGERS BACK IN '73.

HOW?

PLAYIN' WITH GUNS.

OF COURSE.

31

CAPTAIN HALE?

YES, SIR?

YOUR MEN ARE ORDERED TO **CAMBRIDGE**. YOU WILL BE STATIONED ON **WINTER HILL**.

"WINTER HILL"? SOUNDS COZY.

I HOPE CAMBRIDGE IS A LITTLE LESS CROWDED.

BOOOM

AND A LITTLE LESS DANGEROUS!

ANOTHER 12-POUNDER, MORE POWDER IN THE CHARGE, THOUGH. **NICE SHOT!**

PHEW! IT'S A LONG MARCH TO CAMBRIDGE.

LOOK AT THESE GUYS.

IS THERE TROUBLE UP AHEAD?

THERE'S TROUBLE EVERYWHERE.

...DON'T WORRY, IT'LL FIND YOU.

WE ARE HEADED TO **WINTER HILL**. IS IT CLOSE?

JUST UP AHEAD. MAKE SURE YOU DON'T GET THE WRONG HILL.

WINTER HILL IS CLOSE TO **BUNKER** HILL—YOU DON'T WANT TO GO THERE.

BUNKER HILL! NOW *THAT* WAS A *BATTLE!*

WE MISSED THAT BATTLE.

WELL *I* DIDN'T! *I* WAS THERE!

YOU FOUGHT AT THE BATTLE OF BUNKER HILL?

YES, I DID!

WAS IT A BIG BATTLE?

AS BIG AS THEY COME!

THERE WERE OVER A THOUSAND REBEL SOLDIERS HOLDING BUNKER HILL...

LET **HALE** TELL IT WITH PICTURES!

I CAN DO PICTURES TOO!

HERE'S BUNKER HILL AND HERE'S BREED'S HILL.

THESE PEBBLES ARE THE REBELS, AND THE ACORNS ARE GENERAL HOWE'S LIGHT INFANTRY!

PLEEEEASE CAN HE TELL IT?

QUIET! THIS ROCK IS BRIGADIER GENERAL PIGOT.

WOOPS! LOOKS LIKE GENERAL PIGOT IS A PILL BUG.

HUSH! THE REBELS HELD THE HILLTOP.

THEY HAD SETTLED IN AT NIGHT AND BUILT FORTIFICATIONS.

PSSSST.

AH!

THE BATTLE OF BUNKER HILL, 1775

THIS IS THE H.M.S. *LIVELY*-- SHE SPOTTED THE REBELS ON THE HILL.

THE REBELS WERE SETTING UP ARTILLERY TO FIRE RIGHT INTO BOSTON.

THE LIVELY STARTED FIRING! POW! POW! POW!

THEN A BUNCH OF OTHER BRITISH SHIPS STARTED FIRING! BOOM! BOOM! BOOM! POW!

BUT THE SHIPS COULDN'T AIM THEIR GUNS **HIGH** ENOUGH TO HIT THE HILLTOP.

HA HA! YOU MISSED!

BAM BOOM BLAM BAM

SO GENERAL HOWE DECIDED TO TAKE THE HILL WITH OUR TROOPS--AN EASY TARGET.

IT WASN'T SO EASY, WAS IT?

I'M GETTING TO THAT!

2,000 BRITISH TROOPS CROSSED THE HARBOR FOR THE ATTACK. HOWE'S TROOPS CAME RIGHT UP THE MIDDLE AND CHARGED BREED'S HILL!

CHARGE!

THE FIRST CHARGE FAILED.

THERE WERE 1,000 REBELS SNIPING AT THEM FROM THE HILLTOP.

LET ME TELL IT!

THAT FIRST CHARGE WAS ONLY A **TEST!**

A PRETTY **DEADLY** TEST.

THE SECOND CHARGE WAS A TEST TOO!

CHARGE!

BY "TEST," DO YOU MEAN "FAILED ATTEMPT"?

QUIET!

THE *THIRD* CHARGE TOOK THE HILL!

CHARGE!

DO YOU KNOW WHY YOU WON ON THE THIRD CHARGE?

SUPERIOR TACTICS!

CHARGING UP HILL INTO ENEMY GUNFIRE IS YOUR IDEA OF SUPERIOR TACTICS?

WE **WON** DIDN'T WE?

THE BRITISH TOOK THE HILL BECAUSE THE AMERICANS *RAN OUT OF AMMO!*

DON'T SHOOT 'TIL YOU SEE THE WHITES OF THEIR EYES!

NONSENSE! THEY RAN BECAUSE THEY WERE BEATEN AND TERRIFIED!

THERE WERE OVER *1,000* BRITISH CASUALTIES.

WHAT'S A "CASUALTY"?

THAT MEANS WOUNDED OR KILLED.

WOW! WHAT A SLAUGHTER!

BUT WE WON!

THE AMERICANS RETREATED DOWN THE BACK OF THE HILL.

WE HAD LESS THAN HALF THE CASUALTIES THE BRITISH DID.

BUT WE WON!

HEY! NOT FAIR! *I* WAS TELLING THIS STORY!

YOU **DID** TELL IT. I JUST HELPED.

WITH BETTER PICTURES!

ENJOY YOUR PICTURES NOW! CAPTAIN HALE ISN'T GOING TO BE AROUND MUCH LONGER!

WHAT WAS SO IMPORTANT ABOUT THIS DUMB HILL?

IT WAS TALL ENOUGH TO SHOOT INTO BOSTON.

IF YOU CONTROLLED THESE HILLS, YOU COULD CONTROL BOSTON CITY AND HARBOR.

BOSTON WAS THE BRITISH ARMY'S BASE. WE WANTED TO KEEP THEM PINNED DOWN.

BUNKER HILL

BREED'S HILL

CHARLESTOWN

BOSTON

TRYING TO KEEP 'EM ALL IN ONE PLACE, EH?

EXACTLY! IT WAS CALLED, "THE SIEGE OF BOSTON."

SOUNDS DANGEROUS!

IT WAS. WE HAD OUR ARMY SPREAD OUT BLOCKING ALL ROADS INTO BOSTON.

WINTER HILL

CAMBRIDGE

CHARLESTOWN

BUNKER HILL

BOSTON

SOME SIEGE! YOU HAD THE LAND, BUT WE RULED THE SEA!

ROXBURY

DORCHESTER HEIGHTS

BUT WE KEPT YOU IN BOSTON!

FOR ELEVEN MONTHS!

FOR A LITTLE WHILE...

ELEVEN LONG, MUDDY, COLD, HUNGRY, NASTY MONTHS!

WINTER HILL, 1776

THIS IS MISERABLE! WHY COULDN'T WE BE STATIONED ON SUMMER HILL?

SO HUNGRY... I WISH WE HAD SOME SUPPLIES.

WHY WAIT FOR SUPPLIES WHEN YOU CAN MAKE YOUR OWN?

I'VE GOT SOME SHOE STEW!

WHO WANTS SOME?

I DO.

YEAH, I'LL TAKE SOME.

CAPTAIN HALE! THEY'VE JUST ATTACKED OUR BASE IN **ROXBURY**!

ROXBURY? WE JUST LEFT THERE!

YOU JUST MISSED IT! THEY BLASTED US WITH ARTILLERY FOR HOURS!

HERE ARE YOUR ORDERS.

WE'RE ORDERED BACK TO ROXBURY--ON THE DOUBLE!

ANY FOOD THERE?

CAN'T BE ANY WORSE THAN HERE.

DOESN'T LOOK ANY WORSE THAN WHEN WE LEFT.

IT MIGHT EVEN LOOK **BETTER**.

CAPTAIN HALE, WE'RE GLAD YOU'RE BACK. **EVERYONE** IS DESERTING!

WASHINGTON'S ARMY IS SHRINKING.

HA! THERE ARE NO DESERTERS IN OUR ARMY.

MANY OF THE BRITISH **WANTED** TO DESERT, BUT THEY WERE STUCK IN BOSTON, FREEZING AND STARVING.

I'D JOIN WHATEVER SIDE OFFERED ME A BIG, JUICY **STEAK**.

DON'T TALK ABOUT FOOD. IT JUST MAKES YOU **HUNGRIER**.

BACK TO WORK, YOU! FINISH TEARING DOWN THAT WALL!

WE NEED IT FOR FIREWOOD!

CHAPTER 5

ZZZZZ

CAPTAIN HALE, CAPTAIN HALE!

WHA-WHAT!?

IS IT AN **ATTACK**?

NO ATTACK-- NO, IT'S A **MIRACLE**!

THE REGIMENT IS SAVED! WE WON'T STARVE TO DEATH!

LOOK OVER THERE!

IT'S A *COW*... IT'S A *MIRACLE* COW!

CAN WE HAVE IT? IT'S NOT OURS...

UH-OH! GET DOWN! BOOOM

WE'RE UNDER ATTACK! STAY DOWN! BUT MY DINNER IS OUT THERE!

HOLD ON, GIRL! YOU'RE COMING WITH ME! BLAM MOO? SARGE!

FOOM

NNNoooooooo!

Dear diary, I saw a cow blasted to bits today...

CALM DOWN, SARGE. IT'S ALL RIGHT. BUT SHE WAS MY MIRACLE COW.

WE ALL MISS THE COW. THERE, THERE. WILL THIS SIEGE EVER END?

POOR MIRACLE COW. DID THE SIEGE EVER END?

IT *DID* END. HOW? THE *GUNS OF* FORT TICONDEROGA.

CHAPTER 6

THIS STORY STARTS WITH A GROUP CALLED "THE GREEN MOUNTAIN BOYS."

WERE THEY A MUSICAL GROUP?

NO, THEY WERE A MILITARY UNIT!

HANGMAN'S RIGHT, IT SOUNDS LIKE A SINGING AND DANCING GROUP.

OH, WE ARE THE GREEN MOUNTAIN BOYS! WE LIKE TO PLAY WITH TOYS...

WE'LL DANCE AND MAKE SOME NOISE!

WE ARE THE GREEEEEN MOUNTAAAAIN BOOOOOYS!

...

FINISHED?

YEAH. WE'RE DONE.

THANK HEAVENS.

THE GREEN MOUNTAIN BOYS WERE LED BY ETHAN ALLEN.

HE HAS TWO FIRST NAMES.

ETHAN AND THE BOYS HAD ONE GOAL: TO KEEP SETTLERS OUT OF VERMONT.

GET OUT OR I'LL BURN YOU OUT!

ESPECIALLY *NEW YORKERS*. HE *HATED* NEW YORKERS.

GO NOW AND COMPLAIN TO THAT **DAMN** SCOUNDREL, YOUR **GOVERNOR**!

I'LL SEND HIS TROOPS *TO HELL*!!!*

*ACTUAL HISTORICAL QUOTE FROM ETHAN ALLEN.

39

WOW! HE *REALLY* DIDN'T LIKE NEW YORKERS.

WHICH SIDE WAS HE ON?

HE WAS ON HIS *OWN* SIDE. HE CAUSED ALL KINDS OF MISCHIEF. THERE WAS AN OPEN WARRANT FOR HIS ARREST-- WITH A $100 REWARD.

ETHAN ALLEN

$100.00 REWARD

SOUNDS LIKE TROUBLE.

SOUNDS LIKE A WEIRDO.

WHEN THE WAR BROKE OUT, ETHAN ALLEN AND THE GREEN MOUNTAIN BOYS JOINED THE FIGHT AGAINST ENGLAND.

DIRTY BRITS!

ENEMY LIST
1. REDCOATS
2. NEW YORKERS
3. SETTLERS
'GOVERNORS
GOPHERS

WE'LL RUN 'EM ALL OFF!

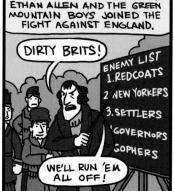

THAT'S WHEN AN AMERICAN COLONEL NAMED BENEDICT ARNOLD SHOWED UP.

MR. ALLEN, DO YOU KNOW LAKE CHAMPLAIN?

BETTER THAN ANY MAN ALIVE!

FORT TICONDEROGA SITS ON THE EDGE OF LAKE CHAMPLAIN -- IT'S A BRITISH FORT.

BUT RIGHT NOW, THE BRITISH ARE FOCUSED ON THE SIEGE OF BOSTON.

I HAVE A BRILLIANT PLAN!

WE COULD *CAPTURE* THAT *FORT!*

WELL, YES. THAT WAS MY IDEA.

WHOSE IDEA?

IT'S..ER...IT'S A GOOD IDEA, WHOEVER HAD IT. I WILL COMMAND THIS MISSION.

WHO WILL?

UH, WE'LL *SHARE* THE COMMAND.

40

EARLY ON THE MORNING OF **MAY 10, 1775,** THE GREEN MOUNTAIN BOYS, LED BY ETHAN ALLEN AND BENEDICT ARNOLD, CROSSED LAKE CHAMPLAIN TO FORT TICONDEROGA.

SSSSSHH. WE WANT TO TAKE 'EM BY SURPRISE!

IT LOOKS EMPTY.

SSSSH! THERE'S ONE SENTRY.

QUIETLY.

QUIETLY.

CHARGE!

HUH?

WHO'S IN CHARGE?

WHERE IS YOUR COMMANDING OFFICER? WE REQUEST HIS IMMEDIATE SURRENDER.

COME OUT OF THERE, YOU DAMNED OLD **RAT!***

*ANOTHER HISTORICAL QUOTE FROM ETHAN ALLEN.

WE HEREBY REQUEST THAT ALL ARMS AND MATERIAL BE REQUIS--

GET OUT OR WE'LL *KILL* EVERYONE IN THIS FORT!!

YES, YES! WE SURRENDER THE FORT!

'BOUT TIME!

I SURRENDER FORT TICONDEROGA TO--

TO ME! ETHAN ALLEN AND THE GREEN MOUNTAIN BOYS!

YEEEEEEHAW!

ACTUALLY TO *ME*, *I'M* THE HIGH-RANKING OFFICER.

LET'S CLAIM OUR FORT, BOYS!

WHOOO! OUR OWN FORT!

WAH HOO!

YAHOOO!

WHERE DID YOU FIND THESE TROOPS?

VERMONT.

FORT TICONDEROGA WAS THE FIRST AMERICAN VICTORY OF THE WAR.

WHAT HAPPENED TO THE GREEN MOUNTAIN BOYS?

WELL, AFTER THEY LIBERATED THE FORT, THEY FOUND THE LIQUOR STORAGE AND LIBERATED THAT TOO.

WE ARE THE GREEEN MOUNTAAAIN BOYS!

HEY LOOK! THEY *ARE* SINGING!

ETHAN ALLEN WAS SO PLEASED WITH HIS VICTORY THAT HE TOOK THE GREEN MOUNTAIN BOYS ON A NEW QUEST.

TAKE CARE OF MY FORT, BENNY. WE'RE GOING TO GO CAPTURE MONTREAL!

GOOD RIDDANCE!

HE WANTED TO CAPTURE A WHOLE CITY?

HE'S A KOOK!

WE DID THIS BEFORE, IT SHOULD WORK AGAIN.

WE'LL CROSS THE RIVER AT NIGHT...

AND SNEAK UP ON 'EM!

SSSH. QUIETLY NOW.

COME ON OUT, YOU DAMN DIRTY RATS!

FIGHT FOR IT, BOYS!

POW
POW
BANG
POW
BLAM
WHAM

ETHAN ALLEN! DO YOU SURRENDER?

NEVER!

BLAM
CRACK
BOOM
POW POW
FWAM

NOW DO YOU SURRENDER!?

OH, ALL RIGHT.

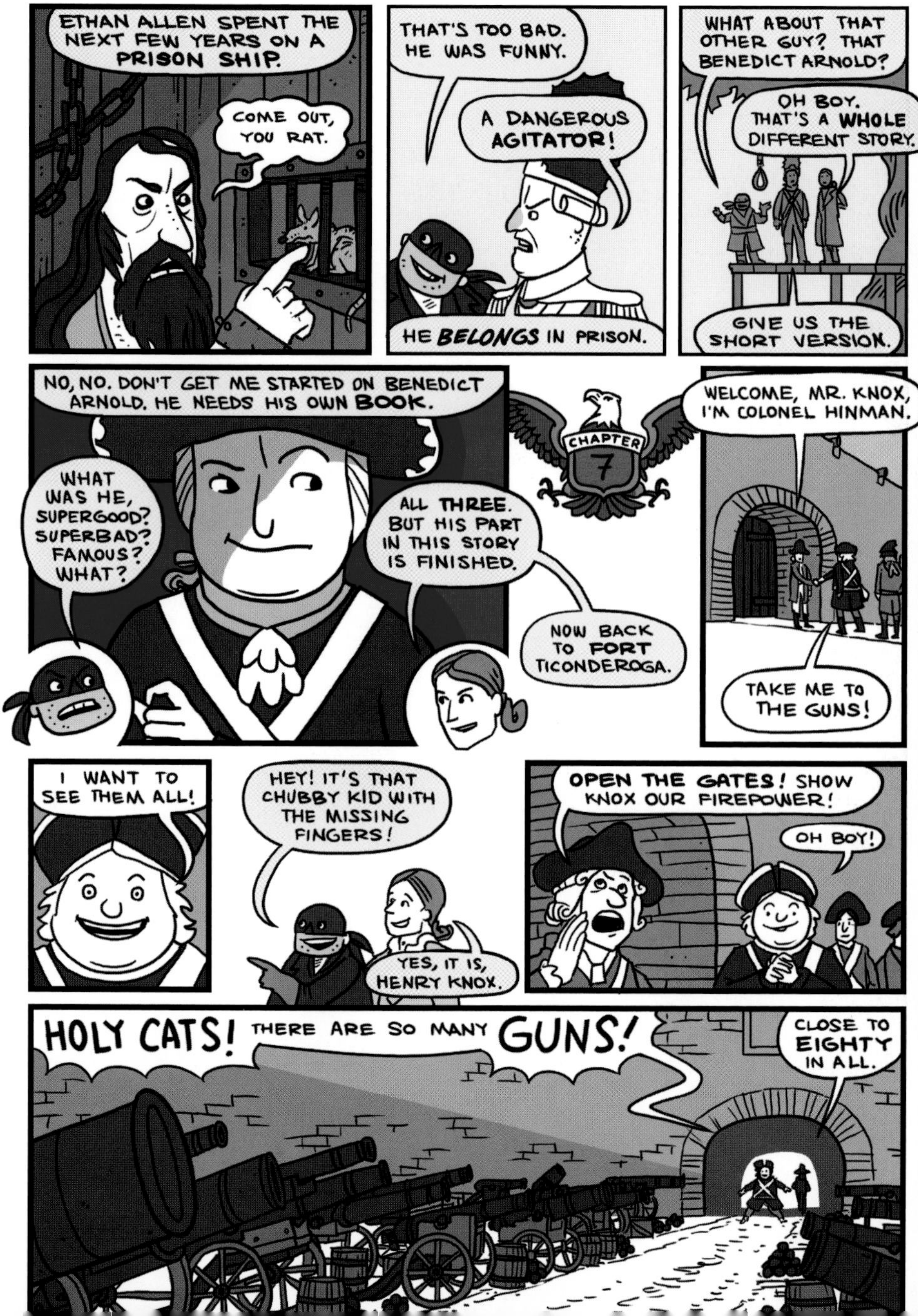
ETHAN ALLEN SPENT THE NEXT FEW YEARS ON A PRISON SHIP.
COME OUT, YOU RAT.
THAT'S TOO BAD. HE WAS FUNNY.
A DANGEROUS AGITATOR!
HE BELONGS IN PRISON.
WHAT ABOUT THAT OTHER GUY? THAT BENEDICT ARNOLD?
OH BOY. THAT'S A WHOLE DIFFERENT STORY.
GIVE US THE SHORT VERSION.
NO, NO. DON'T GET ME STARTED ON BENEDICT ARNOLD. HE NEEDS HIS OWN BOOK.
WHAT WAS HE, SUPERGOOD? SUPERBAD? FAMOUS? WHAT?
ALL THREE. BUT HIS PART IN THIS STORY IS FINISHED.
NOW BACK TO FORT TICONDEROGA.
CHAPTER 7
WELCOME, MR. KNOX, I'M COLONEL HINMAN.
TAKE ME TO THE GUNS!
I WANT TO SEE THEM ALL!
HEY! IT'S THAT CHUBBY KID WITH THE MISSING FINGERS!
YES, IT IS, HENRY KNOX.
OPEN THE GATES! SHOW KNOX OUR FIREPOWER!
OH BOY!
HOLY CATS! THERE ARE SO MANY GUNS!
CLOSE TO EIGHTY IN ALL.

SOME ARE RUSTED, SOME ARE BURIED, BUT 78 ARE READY TO ROLL.

I'LL TAKE SIXTY!

WASHINGTON NEEDS THESE GUNS FOR THE SIEGE OF BOSTON-- AS SOON AS POSSIBLE!

TOO BAD SPRING IS STILL MONTHS AWAY.

I'M NOT WAITING FOR SPRING.

I'LL TAKE THEM NOW.

BUT IT'S DECEMBER.

THE LAKE IS ALMOST FROZEN OVER!

BOSTON IS OVER 300 MILES AWAY!!

LOOK AT THESE BEAUTIES!

THESE ARE LONG RANGE!

IF WE MOUNT THEM JUST RIGHT...

WE COULD SHOOT RIGHT DOWN INTO BOSTON HARBOR!

WE'LL BLAST THEM OUT OF BOSTON!

60 CANNONS WON'T TRAVEL 300 MILES THROUGH THE ICE AND SNOW!

SLEDS!

WE'LL TAKE THE GUNS ON SLEDS!

SLEDS? REALLY? DO YOU HAVE ANY IDEA HOW HEAVY THESE ARE?

DOWN TO THE LAST OUNCE! THIS BABY HERE IS ABOUT 5,000 POUNDS. SHE'S 11 FEET LONG AND CAN FIRE A 24-POUND BALL ABOUT A MILE!

I'LL NAME HER "LUCY"!

I USED TO ONLY **READ** ABOUT GUNS LIKE THIS,

NOW I ACTUALLY GET TO **FIRE** THEM!

60 CANNONS, WHEELS, CARRIAGES, AND SHOT PLUS POWDER EQUALS...

ABOUT **60** TONS.

THERE IS NO WAY YOU CAN HAUL **60** TONS OF *HEAVY METAL* ACROSS LAKE GEORGE *AND* THE HUDSON RIVER IN THE MIDDLE OF **DECEMBER**!!

I'VE GOT BOATS PLANNED FOR THE LAKE, WE BETTER HURRY BEFORE IT FREEZES.

BUT—

THEN I'VE GOT **80** OXEN TO PULL THE SLEDS ON THE OTHER SIDE.

IT WOULD TAKE *MONTHS!*

I TOLD GENERAL WASHINGTON I'D DELIVER 'EM IN **TWO** WEEKS.

YOU ARE OUT OF YOUR MIND.

THESE GUNS WILL **WIN** US THE WAR!

FINE! TAKE THEM! BUT IF YOU WERE **SMART**, YOU'D WAIT UNTIL SPRING!

LET'S LOAD 'EM UP!

QUICK! WE'VE GOT TO GET THEM INTO THE BARGE BEFORE THE LAKE FREEZES SOLID!

WE'LL BUILD THE CRANE HERE.

HEAVE!

ONLY **59** MORE TO GO.

WHAT A SIGHT! ALL THOSE GUNS IN ONE BARGE!

WE'LL SCOUT THE WAY IN THE LITTLE BOAT.

ICE CHUNKS EVERYWHERE!

HOLY SMOKES! WE'RE CROSSING JUST IN TIME!

WE MADE IT! BUT WHERE'S THE BARGE?

WHERE'S THE BARGE!?

PLEASEDON'TBESUNKPLEASEDON'TBESUNKPLEASEDON'TBESUNKPLEASEDON'TBESUNK–

A **ROWBOAT**!?

SHE SUNK! THE BARGE IS GOIN' DOWN!

WHAT!?

TAKE ME TO HER!

SHE'S STILL ABOVE WATER!

WON'T BE FOR LONG!

WHAT HAPPENED?!

WE MUST'VE HIT AN ICE CHUNK!

WE CAN'T LET THIS BARGE SINK!

WE *MIGHT* BE ABLE TO GET TO THAT ISLAND.

DO IT!

WE'D JUST BE **STUCK** OVER THERE.

WE CAN PATCH HER UP AND BAIL HER OUT!

WE CAN *TRY*...

BUT IT WON'T BE *EASY*!

WE HAVE NO CHOICE!

WE **HAVE** TO SAVE THESE **GUNS**!

PATCH! PATCH! PATCH!

BAIL! BAIL! BAIL!

IT WORKED! WE'RE AFLOAT!

NO TIME TO CELEBRATE! WE'VE GOT TO *MOVE* BEFORE WE *FREEZE* INTO THE *ICE*!

48

FINALLY, SAFELY ACROSS! LET'S GET THESE CANNONS ASHORE!

IT'S OXEN TIME!

THE REST OF THIS TRIP SHOULD BE EASY!

HEAVE HEAVE!

I WISH THIS SNOW WOULD STOP!

A LITTLE SNOW CAN'T HURT US!

THE SNOW JUST MAKES THE SLEDS RIDE EASY!

HA HA! JUST A LITTLE FLURRY.

OKAY-- THAT'S ENOUGH SNOW!

BRRRR-R-R-R! SO COLD!

THE COLD IS GOOD NEWS!

IT MEANS WE CAN CROSS THE HUDSON ON THE ICE.

WOW!

NOTHING SLOWS THIS GUY DOWN!

GO HENRY KNOX!

WHAT WERE YOU DOING DURING ALL OF THIS?

I WAS SIEGING BOSTON, REMEMBER?

OH YEAH. WHAT IS SIEGING LIKE? IS IT FUN?

IT'S LIKE THIS:

NO MOVEMENT TODAY.

NO MOVEMENT TODAY.

LEMME GUESS, NO MOVEMENT TODAY?

YOU GOT IT.

SO IT WAS SUPER-BORING?

IT WAS INCREDIBLY BORING!!

MOST OF WAR IS WAITING.

ALL SOLDIERS KNOW THAT.

BUT I WANTED TO FIGHT, OR DO SOMETHING HEROIC LIKE HENRY KNOX!

AND SPEAKING OF HENRY KNOX...

THERE IT IS! THE HUDSON RIVER!

WE'RE ALMOST HOME!

IT'S FROZEN, BUT IS IT FROZEN ENOUGH?

THUMP THUMP

SLOWLY... SLOWLY... CAREFUL...

CREEEEEEEAK

CRACK

BACK UP! BACK UP!

THE ICE IS TOO THIN!

TOO FROZEN FOR A BOAT-- NOT FROZEN ENOUGH TO CROSS ON FOOT!

HOW ARE WE GONNA BEAT THIS RIVER?

50

WE'RE SO CLOSE, BUT SO FAR!

ALL THIS WAY FOR NOTHIN'!

PTEW

COLD ENOUGH TO FREEZE MY SPIT BUT NOT THE RIVER.

HMM...

HEY, THAT GIVES ME AN IDEA!

A SPIT BRIDGE?

I DON'T THINK WE HAVE ENOUGH SPIT.

NO, NOT SPIT-- WATER!

WHAT IF WE POUR WATER ON TOP OF THE ICE?

WOULDN'T IT FREEZE THICKER ON TOP?

WOULD THAT WORK?

WE'VE GOT TO TRY!

GET SOME BUCKETS!

WE'RE GOING TO STRENGTHEN THE ICE WITH ICE!

WHERE SHOULD WE GET THE WATER FROM?

FROM THE RIVER!

BREAK THE ICE!

I THOUGHT WE WERE TRYING TO STRENGTHEN THE ICE.

WE ARE!

NOW SMASH THE ICE!

IT'S WORKING! WE'RE MAKING THE ICE THICKER!

SPLISH

SPLASH

SLOSH

I DON'T BELIEVE THIS!

OKAY, LET'S TRY THIS AGAIN.

I HOPE WE MADE IT THICK ENOUGH!

IT'S WORKING!

IMPOSSIBLE! I STILL DON'T BELIEVE IT!

THAT'S THE LAST OF THEM! OUR ICE BRIDGE DID THE TRICK!

NOT SO FAST, THE BIG GUN ISN'T ACROSS YET. LUCY'S STILL ON THE ICE.

CRACK

SPLASH

NO! LUCY!

TOO BAD.

AT LEAST ALL THE OTHERS MADE IT.

WE AREN'T LEAVING LUCY AT THE BOTTOM OF THE RIVER!

WE AREN'T?

NOT ON MY WATCH!

BUILD A FIRE.

WE'RE GOING FOR A SWIM!

GULP WE ARE?

LATER...

C-C-C-OLD-D-D...

CHEER UP, SOLDIER! WE SAVED LUCY! ALL THE GUNS ARE SAFELY ACROSS!

AS SOON AS WE'RE DRY, WE'LL MOVE OUT!

BOSTON'S CLOSE! WE'VE JUST GOT TO CROSS A MOUNTAIN RANGE OR TWO.

JANUARY 25, 1776

CHAPTER 8

I'M TIRED OF THIS SIEGE! IF I'D KNOWN IT WOULD BE THIS MUCH TROUBLE, I WOULD HAVE MOVED TO THE BACKWOODS AND LIVED IN A WIGWAM!

GENERAL WASHINGTON, SIR, SOMEONE'S COMING.

WHY, IT'S YOUNG HENRY KNOX-- AND HE'S GOT THE GUNS!

GENERAL WASHINGTON, SIR, I PRESENT TO YOU THE GUNS OF FORT TICONDEROGA!

BEAUTIFUL!

KNOX-- KNOX THE OX! BOY, AM I GLAD TO SEE YOU!

THANK YOU, SIR.

CAN WE GO SHOOT THE BRITISH WITH THESE GUNS, SIR?

YES, WE CAN!

YOU THERE, CAPTAIN, GET YOUR MEN TO HELP MOVE THESE CANNONS!

YES, SIR!

HEY, HENRY!

HEY, CAPTAIN NATHAN HALE! I TOLD YOU I HAD A PLAN!

CAN YOU BELIEVE ALL THESE GUNS? MERRY CHRISTMAS TO US!

HA-HA! CHRISTMAS WAS A MONTH AGO!

WAS IT?

LET'S GET THESE GUNS INTO POSITION ON ALL OF OUR HILLTOPS!

WE'LL GIVE THEM A BOMBARDMENT TONIGHT!

WON'T THOSE LOBSTERBACKS BE SURPRISED!

GUNNERS, TAKE YOUR POSITIONS!

FIRE!

KRACK

OH *NO!*

WHAT HAPPENED!?

THE GUNS MUST BE *TOO COLD!*

THIS ONE SHATTERED LIKE *GLASS!*

HOW'S THE RANGE? DID WE HIT ANYTHING?

NO HITS, WE'RE STILL TOO FAR OUT OF RANGE.

WE'RE JUST NOT CLOSE ENOUGH TO HIT BOSTON.

THEN WE'LL HAVE TO MOVE IN A BIT *CLOSER.*

WHERE?

DORCHESTER HEIGHTS! RIGHT UP THERE.

WHAT'S ON THOSE HILLS, CAPTAIN HALE?

JUST A FEW HOUSES, BUT THE BRITISH BURNED THEM ALL DOWN. THOSE HILLS ARE UNFORTIFIED.

SO, LET'S GO *FORTIFY THEM!*

YES, SIR!

MARCH 4, 1776 SIX WEEKS LATER.

WE'VE GOT THE GUNS, WE'VE SCOUTED THE HILL, IT'S TIME TO **BLAST** THE BRITISH OUT OF BOSTON!

TONIGHT IS THE NIGHT WE BUILD OUR FORT ON THE HEIGHTS!

WE MUST SURPRISE THEM!

THEN IT'S ARTILLERY **TIME!**

A STROKE WELL AIMED AT THIS CRITICAL JUNCTURE MIGHT PUT A FINAL END TO THE WAR.

WE'RE GOING TO **BUILD** THE FORT DOWN HERE.

THEN **MOVE** IT UP THE HILL.

DORCHESTER HEIGHTS

YES, **SIR!**

KEEP CHOPPING! WE NEED ALL THE WOOD WE CAN GET!

CHOP CHOP

CHOP

I SAY, DO YOU HEAR CHOPPING?

I HEAR NOTHING OF THE SORT.

CHOP CHOP CHOP

DOES HE **REALLY** WANT US TO BUILD THE FORT DOWN HERE?

THAT'S THE PLAN.

WE'LL BUILD IT ALL IN **PIECES,** LITTLE MINI-FORTS. THEY'RE CALLED "CHANDELIERS."

THIS CHANDELIER IS FINISHED!

LONG NIGHT...

ON WASHINGTON'S SIGNAL, EVERYONE MOVE YOUR CHANDELIER INTO POSITION.

YAWN

SCRITCH SCRITCH

🎵

STRETCH

BLIMEY!

WHERE DID THAT **FORT** COME FROM?

WHO WAS STANDING GUARD?

IT WASN'T THERE A MINUTE AGO!

IF THEY GET ANY LARGE GUNS UP THERE WE'LL BE IN BIG TROUBLE!

BOOM

BOOM BOOM

WE'RE IN BIG TROUBLE.

IT'S TIME TO BRING ON A **RUMPUS!**

56

DO YOU KNOW WHAT GENERAL HOWE, THE BRITISH COMMANDER, SAID THAT MORNING?

NO, BUT I'M SURE YOU'LL TELL US...

HE SAID:

MY GOD, THESE FELLOWS HAVE DONE MORE WORK IN ONE NIGHT THAN I COULD MAKE MY ARMY DO IN **THREE MONTHS!**

HE DID NOT SAY THAT!

THAT'S AN EXACT QUOTE.

BOOM BOOM BOOOM

FROM OUR NEW FORT ON DORCHESTER HEIGHTS, WE *RAINED* FIRE DOWN ON BOSTON.

SO *LOUD!*

DIG IN! THEY'LL BE SHOOTING BACK AT US SOON!

I CAN'T DIG IN! THE GROUND'S FROZEN!

BOOM

INCOMING, KNOX! GET **DOWN!**

NO NEED! I HAVE A THEORY ABOUT THEIR ARTILLERY!

GET **DOWN** AND TELL US YOUR THEORY.

BY STANDING UP, I'LL **PROVE** MY THEORY!

HAHA! I *KNEW* IT!

WE'RE **TOO** HIGH TO **HIT!**

FOOM

KROOM KROM KROOM

CAN'T THEY AIM HIGHER?

NOPE, THAT'S AS HIGH AS THEY CAN AIM THEIR GUNS.

THEY CAN'T HIT US?

NO, BUT *WE* CAN HIT *THEM!*

BEE-YOO-TI-FUL!

BUNKER HILL

BREEDS HILL

BOSTON

ROXBURY NECK

DORCHESTER HEIGHTS

IT ALMOST SEEMS *TOO* EASY!

HEY! THERE WAS *NOTHING* EASY ABOUT GETTING THESE GUNS.

OR BUILDING THIS **FORT!**

LOOK! THE SHIPS ARE SAILING AWAY!

I DON'T BELIEVE IT! THE BRITISH ARE LEAVING **BOSTON!**

THE SIEGE IS **OVER!**

WE WON!

HOORAY!

NONSENSE!

WE LEFT BOSTON BECAUSE WE *FELT LIKE IT!*

YOUR GUNS AND SILLY OVERNIGHT FORT HAD **NOTHING** TO DO WITH IT.

THERE WAS A **STORM** MOVING IN, WE LEFT BECAUSE OF **THAT.**

YOU GAVE UP YOUR HARD-FOUGHT POSITIONS FOR A **STORM?**

YES!

WE ENGLISH DON'T... ...LIKE STORMS.

YEAH, CANNONBALL STORMS.

CHAPTER 9

WELL, MEN, SHOULD WE GO VISIT THE CITY WE SPENT THE LAST ELEVEN MONTHS SIEGING?

I'VE NEVER SEEN BOSTON FROM THE INSIDE.

WE LIBERATED THE CITY! THEY'LL PROBABLY SHOWER US WITH FLOWERS!

I'D RATHER BE SHOWERED WITH **FOOD!**

WOO! WHAT A PARTY!

THEY LOVE US!

I'M JUST GOING TO OPEN MY MOUTH AND HOPE SOMEONE THROWS SOME **FOOD** IN IT!

London Bookstore *Cornhill* Boston
HENRY KNOX,
ALSO

HEY, LOOK! HERE'S HENRY'S BOOKSHOP.

IT **WAS** MY SHOP...

IT'S BEEN DESTROYED.

ALL MY BOOKS ARE **GONE**.

SORRY TO HEAR THAT.

DON'T WORRY ABOUT IT. I'M NOT STAYING HERE.

WASHINGTON IS SENDING ME TO **NEW YORK**. I'M IN CHARGE OF SETTING UP OUR ARTILLERY THERE.

WOW! BUT YOU JUST GOT HERE.

HAVEN'T YOU HEARD? WE'RE **ALL** HEADED TO NEW YORK.

WE'VE GOT TO GET THERE BEFORE THE BRITISH DO.

IT'S A **RACE**. WHOEVER GETS THERE FIRST WILL HAVE THE CITY AS THEIR **BASE**.

HEAR THAT? WE'RE GOING TO NEW YORK!

BUT THE PARTY JUST STARTED!

PARTY'S OVER, SON. DON'T YOU KNOW THERE'S A WAR ON?

59

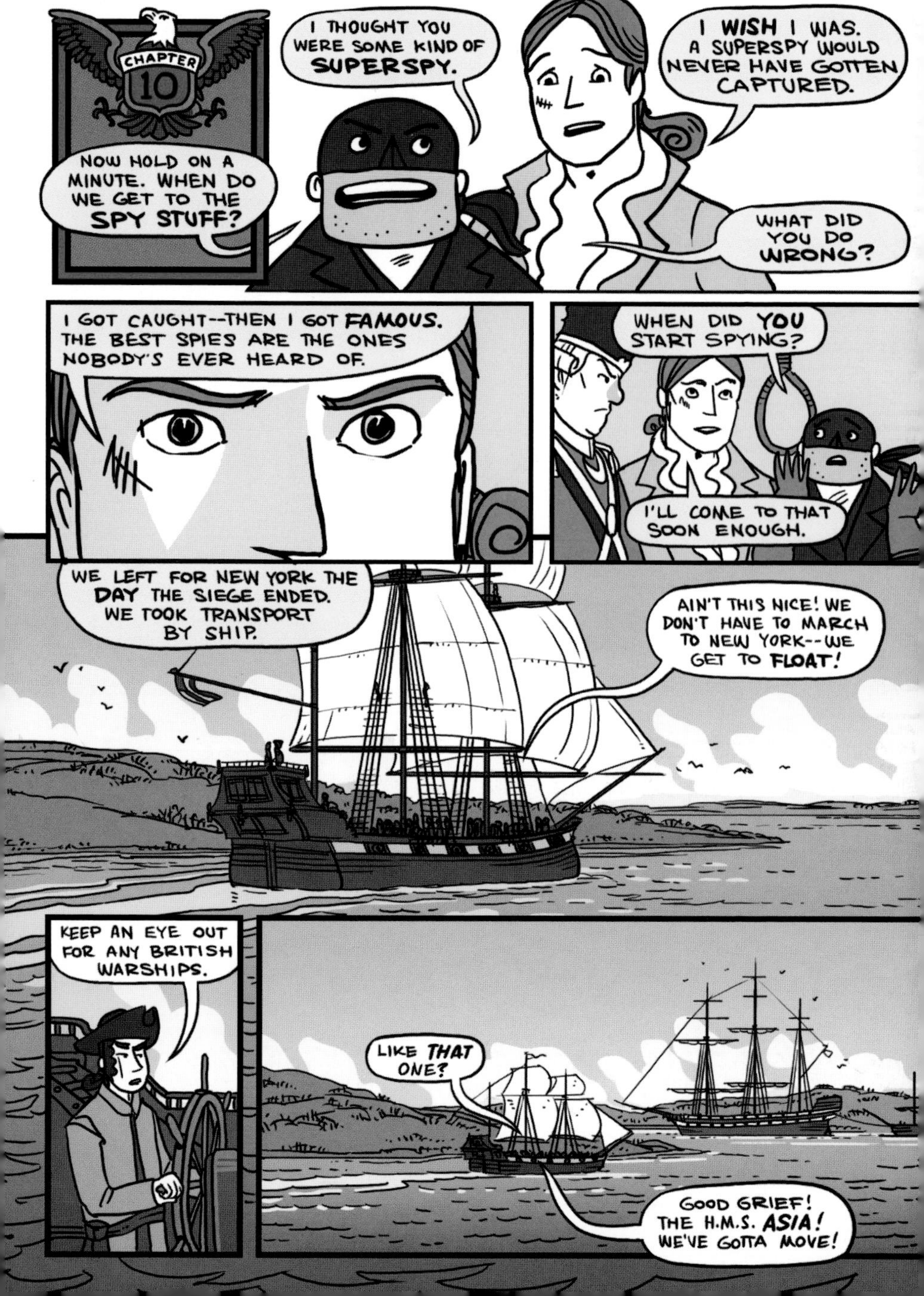
CHAPTER 10
NOW HOLD ON A MINUTE. WHEN DO WE GET TO THE SPY STUFF?
I THOUGHT YOU WERE SOME KIND OF SUPERSPY.
I WISH I WAS. A SUPERSPY WOULD NEVER HAVE GOTTEN CAPTURED.
WHAT DID YOU DO WRONG?
I GOT CAUGHT--THEN I GOT FAMOUS. THE BEST SPIES ARE THE ONES NOBODY'S EVER HEARD OF.
WHEN DID YOU START SPYING?
I'LL COME TO THAT SOON ENOUGH.
WE LEFT FOR NEW YORK THE DAY THE SIEGE ENDED. WE TOOK TRANSPORT BY SHIP.
AIN'T THIS NICE! WE DON'T HAVE TO MARCH TO NEW YORK--WE GET TO FLOAT!
KEEP AN EYE OUT FOR ANY BRITISH WARSHIPS.
LIKE THAT ONE?
GOOD GRIEF! THE H.M.S. ASIA! WE'VE GOTTA MOVE!

LOOK THERE, CLOSE TO THE *ASIA*. DO YOU SEE WHAT I SEE?

THAT LITTLE BOAT?

IT LOOKS LIKE A SUPPLY SHIP--A *FULL* SUPPLY SHIP.

WE SHOULD CAPTURE IT!

THE *ASIA'S* A 64-GUN SHIP OF THE LINE!

THAT'S WHY THEY'D NEVER EXPECT A SNEAK ATTACK FROM A LONE SOLDIER.

IF THERE'S FOOD ON THAT SHIP, COUNT ME IN!

NO MORE SHOE SOUP! FOOD AND AMMO FOR THE WHOLE COMPANY!

WE'LL BE STATIONED IN BROOKLYN -- NOT TOO FAR FROM HERE.

LET'S HIKE BACK HERE WHEN IT GETS DARK.

ALL THAT FOOD -- I CAN PRACTICALLY TASTE IT!

QUIETLY NOW. WE CAN'T ALERT THE *ASIA*!

THAT SHIP WOULD BLOW US TO SMITHEREENS!

AWW. DO WE *HAVE* TO GET WET?

OF COURSE WE DO! WE'RE STEALING A BOAT!

DUCK! THERE'S A WATCHMAN ON THE *ASIA*!

EVERYBODY *FREEZE*!

OH. I'M FREEEZING ALL RIGHT.

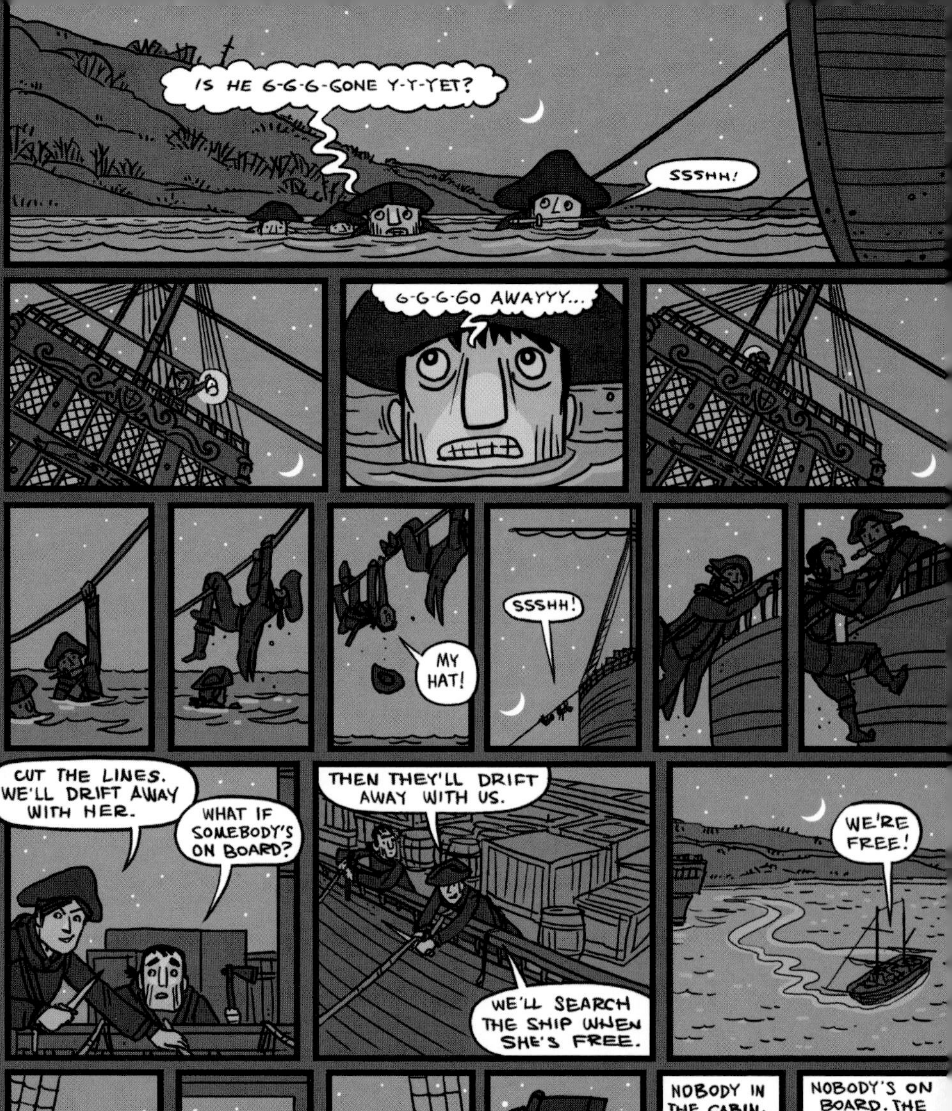
IS HE G-G-G-GONE Y-Y-YET?
SSSHH!
G-G-G-GO AWAYYY...
MY HAT!
SSSHH!
CUT THE LINES. WE'LL DRIFT AWAY WITH HER.
WHAT IF SOMEBODY'S ON BOARD?
THEN THEY'LL DRIFT AWAY WITH US.
WE'LL SEARCH THE SHIP WHEN SHE'S FREE.
WE'RE FREE!
CREAK
RRRRRRR
NOBODY IN THE CABIN.
NOBODY BELOW.
NOBODY'S ON BOARD. THE SHIP IS OURS.
WOOHOO!

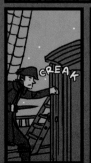

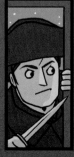

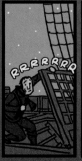

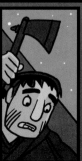

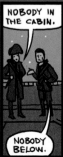

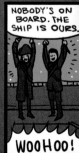

A SHIP'S COMING.

IT'S CAPTAIN HALE!

HALE STOLE A SHIP!

SUPPLIIIIIIIIIES!!!

I'LL HAVE YOU WRITTEN UP FOR THEFT!

HA HA!

ADD IT TO MY LIST.

CHAPTER 11

WE WON THE RACE FOR NEW YORK AND SET TO WORK BUILDING FORTS.

LOTS OF FORTS. WASHINGTON SAID NEW YORK WAS "THE KEY TO THE CONTINENT."

WE COVERED LONG ISLAND IN FORTS.

WHY SO MANY?

WE DIDN'T KNOW WHERE THE BRITISH WOULD LAND.

IT'S AN ISLAND, WE COULD LAND ANYWHERE WE WANTED TO.

EXACTLY. NEW YORK WAS GOING TO BE MUCH TRICKIER THAN BOSTON.

BUILD, BUILD, BUILD! DIG, DIG, DIG!

IT'S LIKE DORCHESTER HEIGHTS EVERY DAY!

HO THERE! NATHAN HALE?

BEN? BEN TALLMADGE FROM YALE?

YOU FINALLY JOINED THE WAR, HUH?

SURE DID. HOW ARE YOU, YOU OLD WINDOW SMASHER?

I'M GOOD. DIGGING TRENCHES, HOW ABOUT YOU?

I'M WONDERFUL!

HAVE YOU HEARD THE NEWS?

WHAT NEWS?

THEY'VE DECLARED INDEPENDENCE!

WHO DID WHAT?

CONGRESS-- THE FELLOWS IN PHILADELPHIA, THEY'VE MADE IT OFFICIAL.

WE'RE OUR OWN COUNTRY NOW.

HOW'D THEY DO THAT?

THEY WROTE A PAPER. IT'S CALLED "THE DECLARATION OF INDEPENDENCE!"

SO.? I DON'T CARE ABOUT NO PAPER. I DOUBT THE REDCOATS DO EITHER.

WOW. INDEPENDENCE.

I'D LOVE TO READ IT.

THEY'LL BE GATHERING THE REGIMENTS TONIGHT.

WASHINGTON IS GOING TO READ IT ALOUD TO ALL OF US.

THAT SOLDIER IS RIGHT. WE DON'T CARE ABOUT YOUR PAPER.

THE HISTORY BOOKS DO. THEY MAKE A HUGE DEAL ABOUT IT.

WHO CARES? IT'S JUST A PAPER.

THE SIGNING OF THE DECLARATION OF INDEPENDENCE WILL BE TAUGHT IN EVERY CLASSROOM IN AMERICA.

WHAT A **SNOOZE**. LET'S GET BACK TO THE WAR STORIES.

YOU SHOULD WEAR THE FANCY UNIFORM YOUR LADY-FRIEND MADE.

OH, I FORGOT ABOUT THAT.

GIVE ME YOUR SILVER SHOE BUCKLES.

HUH? WHAT FOR?

GOT TO POLISH 'EM UP PRETTY FOR THE GENERAL.

I THOUGHT YOU DIDN'T CARE ABOUT "NO PAPER."

YOU'RE THE **CAPTAIN**. YOU'RE THE ONLY ONE OF US WITH A UNIFORM.

YOU STAND IN **FRONT**. YOU HAVE TO LOOK GOOD FOR THE WHOLE COMPANY.

FIX HIS HAIR TOO.

WE DON'T HAVE TIME TO POLISH. WE DON'T WANT TO BE **LATE**!

YOU GO AHEAD AND MARCH. I'LL POLISH THEM AS WE GO.

NO, YOU WON'T!

CUT IT OUT, SARGE!

65

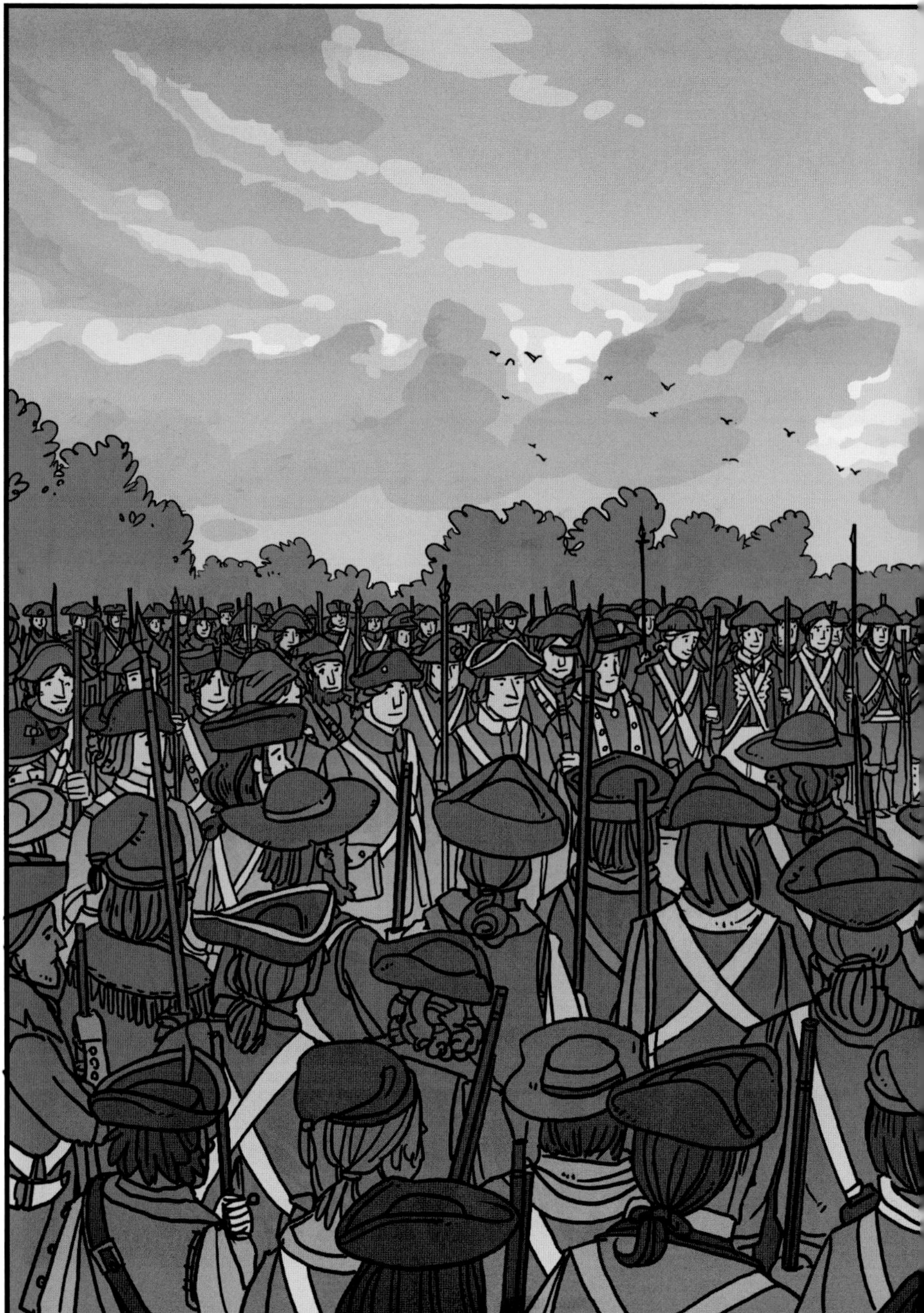

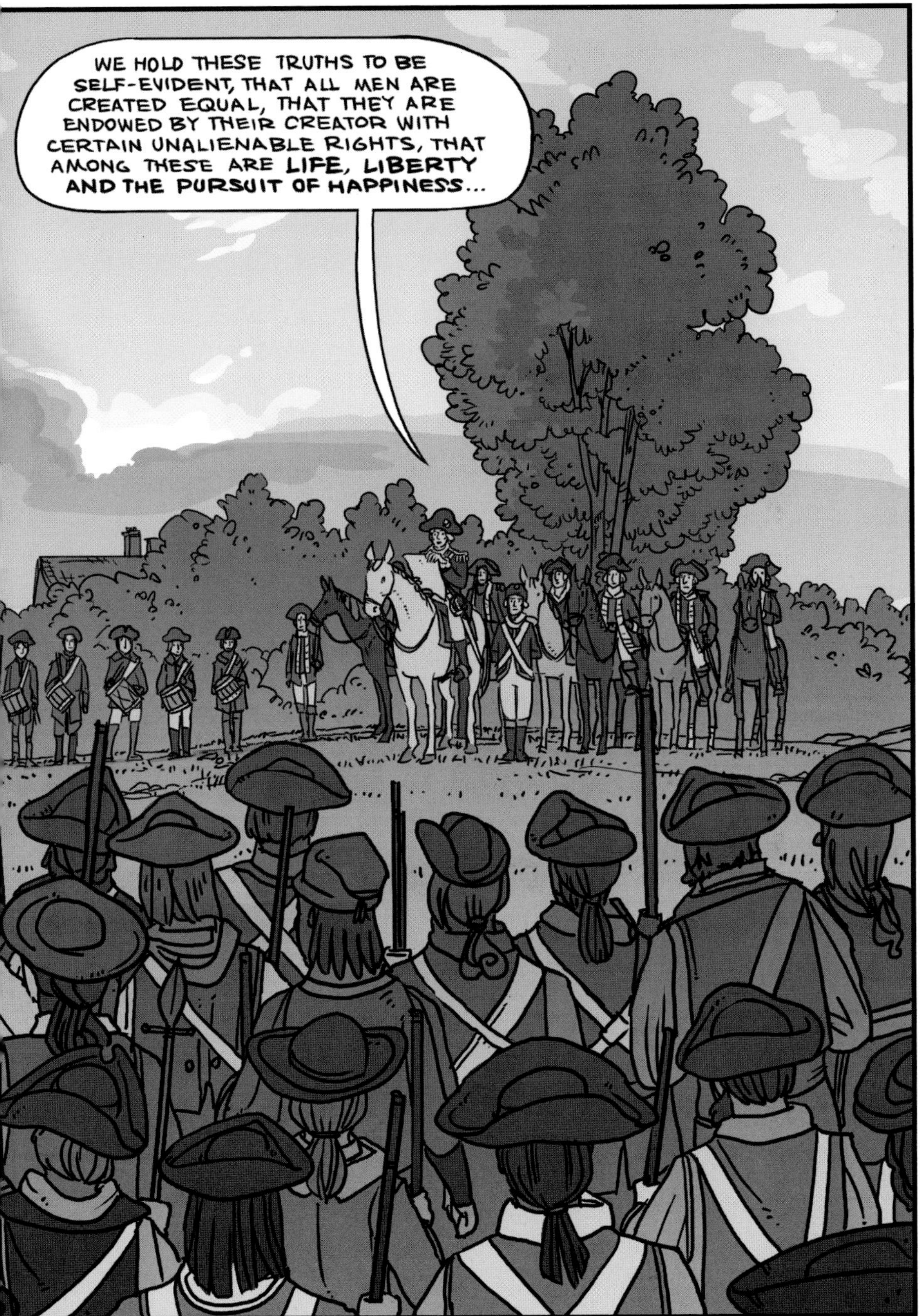
WE HOLD THESE TRUTHS TO BE SELF-EVIDENT, THAT ALL MEN ARE CREATED EQUAL, THAT THEY ARE ENDOWED BY THEIR CREATOR WITH CERTAIN UNALIENABLE RIGHTS, THAT AMONG THESE ARE LIFE, LIBERTY AND THE PURSUIT OF HAPPINESS...

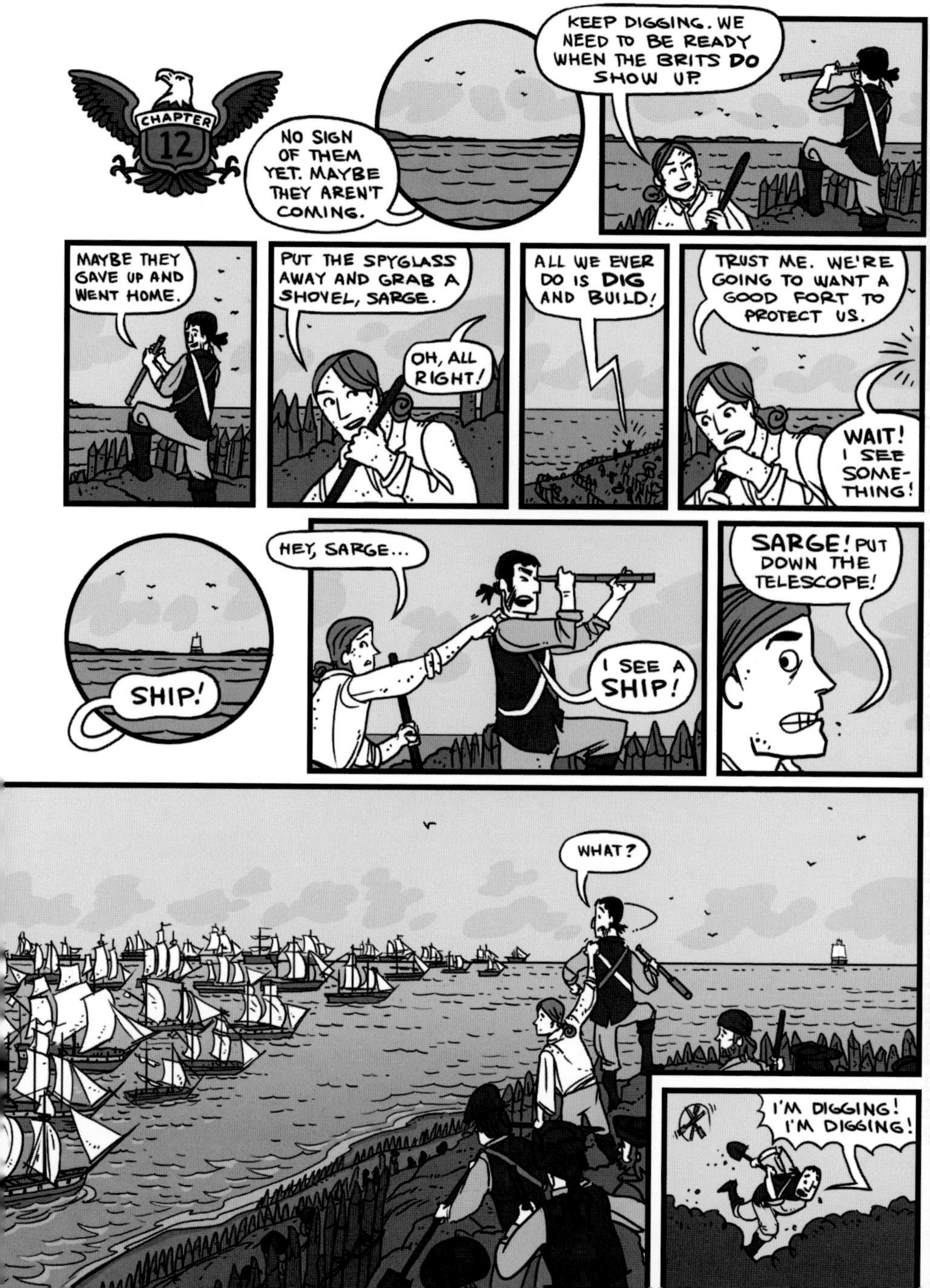
CHAPTER 12
NO SIGN OF THEM YET. MAYBE THEY AREN'T COMING.
KEEP DIGGING. WE NEED TO BE READY WHEN THE BRITS DO SHOW UP.
MAYBE THEY GAVE UP AND WENT HOME.
PUT THE SPYGLASS AWAY AND GRAB A SHOVEL, SARGE.
OH, ALL RIGHT!
ALL WE EVER DO IS DIG AND BUILD!
TRUST ME. WE'RE GOING TO WANT A GOOD FORT TO PROTECT US.
WAIT! I SEE SOME-THING!
SHIP!
HEY, SARGE...
I SEE A SHIP!
SARGE! PUT DOWN THE TELESCOPE!
WHAT?
I'M DIGGING! I'M DIGGING!

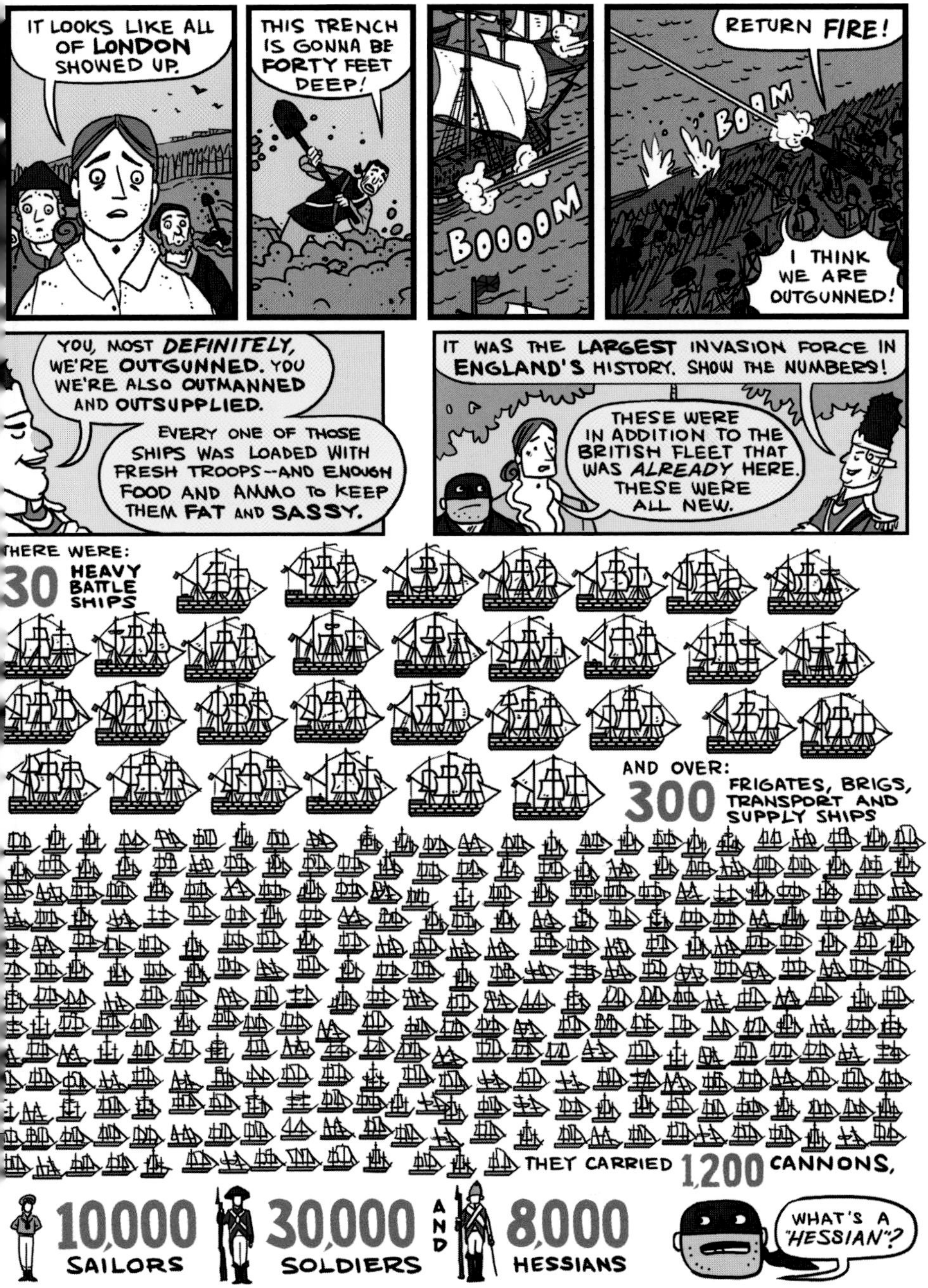

IT LOOKS LIKE ALL OF **LONDON** SHOWED UP.
THIS TRENCH IS GONNA BE **FORTY** FEET DEEP!
BOOOOM
RETURN **FIRE!**
BOOM
I THINK WE ARE OUTGUNNED!
YOU, MOST ***DEFINITELY***, WE'RE **OUTGUNNED.** YOU WE'RE ALSO **OUTMANNED** AND **OUTSUPPLIED.**
EVERY ONE OF THOSE SHIPS WAS LOADED WITH FRESH TROOPS--AND ENOUGH FOOD AND AMMO TO KEEP THEM **FAT** AND **SASSY.**
IT WAS THE **LARGEST** INVASION FORCE IN **ENGLAND'S** HISTORY. SHOW THE NUMBERS!
THESE WERE IN ADDITION TO THE BRITISH FLEET THAT WAS *ALREADY* HERE. THESE WERE ALL NEW.
THERE WERE:
30 HEAVY BATTLE SHIPS
AND OVER:
300 FRIGATES, BRIGS, TRANSPORT AND SUPPLY SHIPS
THEY CARRIED 1,200 CANNONS,
10,000 SAILORS
30,000 SOLDIERS
AND
8,000 HESSIANS
WHAT'S A "*HESSIAN*"?

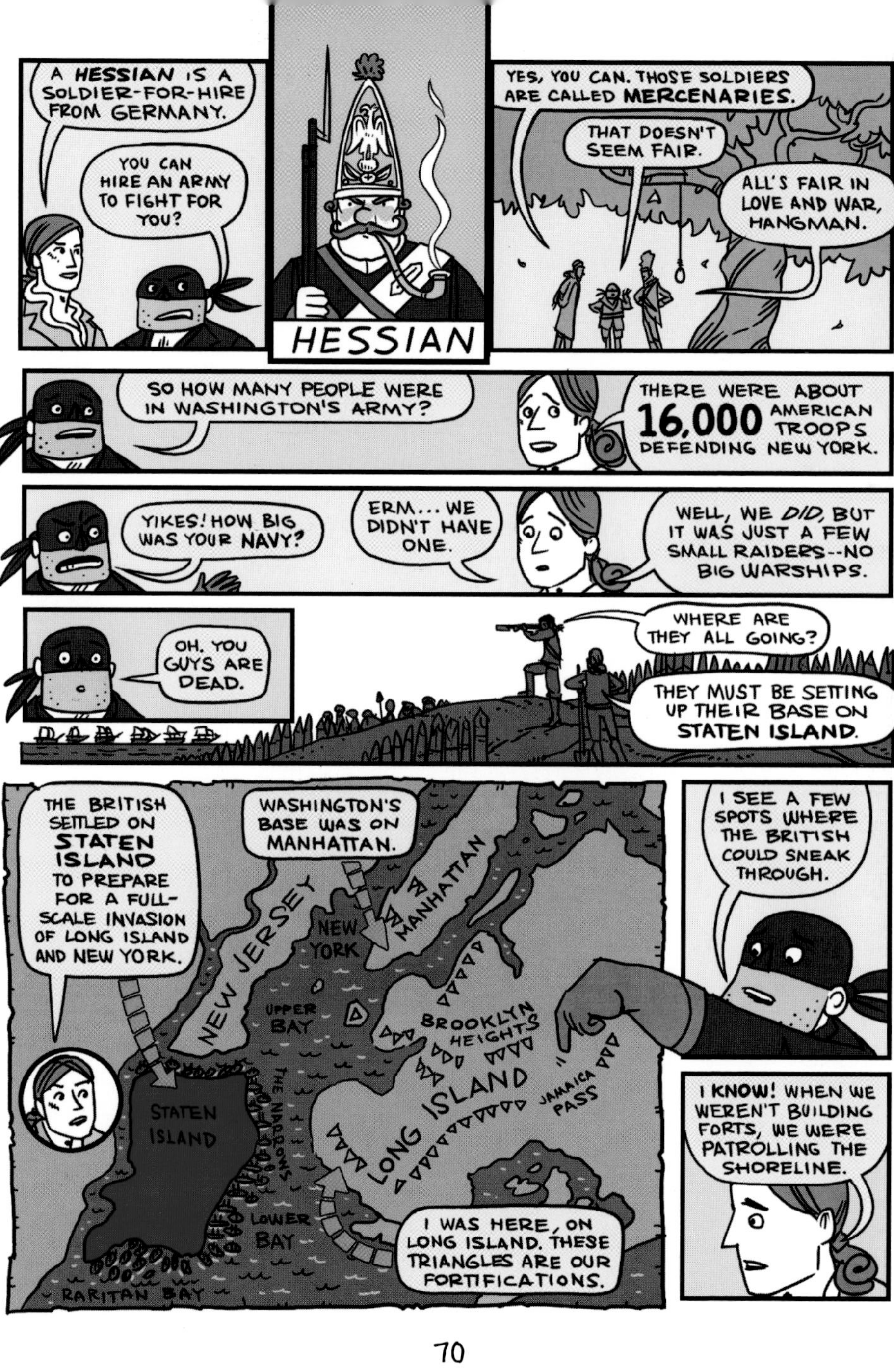

A HESSIAN IS A SOLDIER-FOR-HIRE FROM GERMANY.
YOU CAN HIRE AN ARMY TO FIGHT FOR YOU?
HESSIAN
YES, YOU CAN. THOSE SOLDIERS ARE CALLED MERCENARIES.
THAT DOESN'T SEEM FAIR.
ALL'S FAIR IN LOVE AND WAR, HANGMAN.
SO HOW MANY PEOPLE WERE IN WASHINGTON'S ARMY?
THERE WERE ABOUT 16,000 AMERICAN TROOPS DEFENDING NEW YORK.
YIKES! HOW BIG WAS YOUR NAVY?
ERM... WE DIDN'T HAVE ONE.
WELL, WE DID, BUT IT WAS JUST A FEW SMALL RAIDERS--NO BIG WARSHIPS.
OH, YOU GUYS ARE DEAD.
WHERE ARE THEY ALL GOING?
THEY MUST BE SETTING UP THEIR BASE ON STATEN ISLAND.
THE BRITISH SETTLED ON STATEN ISLAND TO PREPARE FOR A FULL-SCALE INVASION OF LONG ISLAND AND NEW YORK.
WASHINGTON'S BASE WAS ON MANHATTAN.
NEW JERSEY
NEW YORK
MANHATTAN
UPPER BAY
BROOKLYN HEIGHTS
LONG ISLAND
JAMAICA PASS
STATEN ISLAND
THE NARROWS
LOWER BAY
RARITAN BAY
I WAS HERE, ON LONG ISLAND. THESE TRIANGLES ARE OUR FORTIFICATIONS.
I SEE A FEW SPOTS WHERE THE BRITISH COULD SNEAK THROUGH.
I KNOW! WHEN WE WEREN'T BUILDING FORTS, WE WERE PATROLLING THE SHORELINE.

SIR, NORTH PATROL REPORTS MUD, MUD AND MORE **MUD**.

OUR GUNS ARE TOO WET TO SHOOT, AND WE SAW NO SIGN OF ANY BRITISH.

K R A C K

ZOW! THAT WAS CLOSE!

OH **NO!** WHAT HAPPENED TO **SOUTH PATROL?**

YOU DON'T THINK THEY WERE...**STRUCK**...DO YOU?

LET'S GO CHECK. SOMEONE GO FETCH THE **SURGEON!**

THEY DON'T NEED A SURGEON.

DEAD AS DOORNAILS.

KILLED BY LIGHTNING. HOW HORRIBLE.

SHOCKING.

THIS IS NO TIME FOR JOKES. LET'S GO GET SOME STRETCHERS.

HEE-HEE! "SHOCKING."

IT WASN'T FUNNY THEN AND IT ISN'T FUNNY NOW!

WE LOST MEN IN THOSE STORMS TOO.

IT WAS A HARD SUMMER. WHEN IT WASN'T BLAZING HOT, IT WAS POURING RAIN.

71

LOOK SHARP! GENERAL WASHINGTON'S COMING.

HE COMES BY EVERY DAY. WHY DO WE ALWAYS HAVE TO *"LOOK SHARP"*?

BECAUSE *HE* ALWAYS LOOKS SHARP.

HE SURE DOES. HOW DOES HE DO IT?

GOOD EVENING, MEN.

DISCIPLINE, MORE THAN NUMBERS, GIVES ONE ARMY SUPERIORITY OVER ANOTHER.

ARE YOU DISCIPLINED?

YES, SIR!

DOING OUR BEST, SIR.

EXCELLENT! KEEP YOUR POWDER DRY!

YES, SIR!

HOW DOES HE STAY SO CONFIDENT? I WOULDN'T BE IF I WAS IN CHARGE OF THIS MESS.

HE MUST KNOW SOMETHING WE DON'T.

HEY, IT'S OLD BEN *TALLMADGE!*

HEY, NATE! I BROUGHT SOME CARDS. WANNA PLAY?

HOW ABOUT A GAME FOR OLD TIME'S SAKE?

THUMP

HI-YAAAAGH!

CHOP

NOW THAT'S WHAT I CALL *"CUTTING THE CARDS!"*

72

HE WON'T LET **ANYONE** PLAY CARDS HERE.

WE'VE LOST MORE CARDS THAT WAY...

HE WON'T?

I CAN'T LET THEM SEE HOW **BAD** MY LUCK IS.

UNDERSTOOD. CHECKERS THEN?

HOW HAVE YOU BEEN?

GREAT! I'M THE REGIMENTAL ADJUTANT NOW!

CLICK

WOW! THAT'S A **BIG** PROMOTION! HAVE YOU SEEN MUCH ACTION?

SURE! HAVEN'T YOU?

NOT REALLY.

YOU HAVEN'T BEEN IN ANY BATTLES!?

NOPE. THEY ALWAYS SEEM TO HAPPEN WHERE I'M **NOT**.

I HELPED BUILD THE DORCHESTER HEIGHTS FORTS. I'VE USED MY **SHOVEL** MORE THAN MY **MUSKET**.

NICE WORK ON THAT OVERNIGHT FORT.

OH, AND I DID STEAL THAT SUPPLY SHIP.

NOW **THAT** WAS A LUCKY THING!

THAT, PLUS MISSING ALL THE BATTLES SOUNDS LUCKY TO ME.

MAYBE YOUR BAD LUCK HAS CHANGED.

BUT I DON'T **WANT** TO MISS THE BATTLES.

I WANNA **FIGHT**!

YOU'LL GET YOUR CHANCE. WE ALL WILL BEFORE THIS IS OVER.

I JUST WISH THERE WAS SOMETHING I COULD DO.

THERE MIGHT BE.

WHO'S THERE?

CRACK

THOMAS KNOWLTON.

73

COLONEL KNOWLTON! SIR!

HAVE A SEAT.

ACTUALLY, I HAVE TO GET BACK TO MY REGIMENT.

WE'LL FINISH OUR GAME LATER.

WHAT CAN I DO FOR YOU, COLONEL?

I KNOW THAT FACE!

YOU DO?

I SAW HIM...

AT BUNKER HILL!

WAS HE ONE OF THE PEBBLES?

HANG THE PEBBLES!

SHOW BUNKER HILL! THE BATTLE!

LIKE THIS?

CLOSER--THERE ON BREED'S HILL!

THERE HE IS!

CRIKEY! LOOK AT HIM!

HIS MEN STAYED BACK TO GUARD THE AMERICAN RETREAT.

KNOWLTON AND HIS REAR GUARD KILLED MORE ENEMIES THAT DAY THAN ENTIRE BRIGADES DID. *TWICE* AS MANY IN SOME CASES.

YIKES! WHERE'D HE COME FROM?

THOMAS KNOWLTON SERVED **SIX** CAMPAIGNS IN THE FRENCH AND INDIAN WAR...

HE JOINED THE FIGHTING AT AGE FIFTEEN.

IN 1762 HE FOUGHT THE SPANISH IN **CUBA** AND HELPED CAPTURE HAVANA.

HE WENT WITH **107** MEN. BETWEEN THE SPANISH AND YELLOW FEVER, **20** SURVIVED.

THE CAPTURE OF HAVANA WAS A **BRITISH** OPERATION!

HE FOUGHT **WITH** US-- NOW HE FIGHTS **AGAINST** US.

HE'S NOTHING BUT A **TURNCOAT!**

HE WAS A SEASONED WAR HERO! AND HE HAD AN OFFER FOR ME.

I HEARD ABOUT YOUR **BOAT-STEALING** ADVENTURE. NICE WORK!

THANKS! IT WAS EASY, REALLY. THERE WERE HARDLY ANY GUARDS.

BUT TO DO IT ALL IN **SECRET**-- WITHOUT NOISE OR FIGHTING, **THAT** IS IMPRESSIVE.

WASHINGTON WANTS ME TO BUILD AN **ELITE** UNIT--**THE RANGERS.** I WANT **YOU** TO JOIN!

YES, **SIR!**

YOU WOULD STAY A CAPTAIN, BUT YOU WOULD BE A SPECIAL **INTELLIGENCE GATHERER.**

LIKE A **SPY?**

YES.

I'M IN!

EXCELLENT.

CHAPTER 13

WHAT'S GOT EVERYONE SO EXCITED?

HEY THERE, RANGER HALE, DO YOU KNOW WHAT'S GOING ON?

THE INVASION IS *TODAY!*

TODAY? WHERE?

IN BROOKLYN!

10,000 TROOPS WILL BE MARCHING UP THE KING'S HIGHWAY.

WE SPOTTED THEM LAST NIGHT. THEY LANDED AT THE SOUTHERN TIP OF THE ISLAND.

WE'RE *ALL* GOING TO BE FIGHTING TODAY!

CAPTAIN HALE--YOU ARE SCOUTING TODAY.

SCOUTING?

WON'T WE BE FIGHTING WITH THE MAIN FORCE?

YOU ARE AN *INTELLIGENCE OFFICER.* I NEED YOU UP HIGH -- GATHERING INFORMATION FOR THE GENERALS.

WE NEED TO KNOW *EVERYTHING* ABOUT THE ENEMY TROOPS.

YES, SIR, EVERYTHING.

SCOUTING?! WOW! I WAS WRONG ABOUT YOUR LUCK--YOU MAY BE THE **LUCKIEST** GUY I KNOW!

GO SHOOT SOME LOBSTERBACKS FOR ME, BEN.

FOR OUR GLORIOUS COUNTRY!

GOOD LUCK, NATE!

GOOD LUCK TO YOU, BEN!

WELL, SARGE, LET'S GO SCOUT THE ENEMY.

LEAD THE WAY.

HOW DO THEY FIT ALL THOSE LITTLE BOATS INTO THE BIG BOATS?

THERE ARE **SO MANY**! KEEP COUNTING, WE NEED TO GET THEIR NUMBERS RIGHT.

THIS WILL BE THE BIGGEST BATTLE OF THE WAR. DON'T YOU WISH WE COULD BE DOWN THERE?

NO WAY! I'M FINE UP HERE!

ENEMY SCOUTS! GET DOWN!

LOOKS LIKE WE'LL BE FIGHTING AFTER ALL.

LET THEM GET A BIT CLOSER...

NOW!

KRACK

THEY'RE RUNNING!

RELOADING!

KRACK

THEY'RE GONE!

WE MUST REPORT OUR INFO TO THE FRONT LINES!

YOU JUST GOT YOURSELF A LITTLE **WAR** TATTOO.

HUH?

POWDER BURN. YOU HELD YOUR MUSKET TOO CLOSE TO YOUR FACE.

BETTER THAN A RED BADGE!

LET'S MOVE BEFORE WE GET PINNED WITH ONE OF THOSE!

I WANT A RED BADGE!

YOU WANT TO GET **SHOT**? A "RED BADGE" IS A BULLET HOLE.

I DO **NOT** WANT A RED BADGE.

BEN TALLMADGE NEARLY EARNED A RED BADGE THAT DAY.

HERE THEY COME!

PREPA-A-A-RE **ARMS!**

PREPA-A-A-RE **ARMS!**

READY... AIM...

READY... AIM...

FIRE!

POW BAM KRACK

KRACK POW KRACK

FIRE!

HOLD STEADY! *FIRE!*

POW POW KRACK

SIR! WORD FROM **THE SCOUTS**; A SECOND ARMY IS COMING FROM OUR REAR!

WHAT? HOW DID THEY GET THROUGH?

HOLD STEADY!

TWO ARMIES! RUN! RUN!

RUN! RUN!

SPIES FOR THE BRITISH HAD LED GENERAL HOWE THROUGH AN UNGUARDED PASS WITH 10,000 MEN.

GOWANUS CREEK

SWAMP

JAMAICA PASS

HOWE'S 10,000

LONG ISLAND

WOOPS.

OUR MAIN FORCE WAS NOW TRAPPED BETWEEN *TWO* ARMIES!

RETREAT!

THROUGH THE **SWAMP**! IT'S THE ONLY WAY!

FOLLOW ME!

MARYLAND TROOPS! STAND WITH ME! WE'LL ATTACK NEAR THAT OLD STONE HOUSE!

RUN, BOYS! WE'LL TRY TO BUY YOU SOME TIME!

ATTACK!

RETREAT! TO THE HEIGHTS!

THOSE MARYLAND BOYS ARE BRAVE!

HESSIANS!

GRRRR!

SLASH

GET US OUT OF HERE, GIRL!

BLAM

KEEP RUNNING, GIRL.

TAKE US TO THE BROOKLYN HEIGHTS!

DID I HIT ANYTHING?

CHAPTER 14

THE BATTLE OF LONG ISLAND WAS THE BIGGEST OF THE WAR. OVER 40,000 MEN FOUGHT THAT DAY.

SO MUCH FOR ALL OF OUR DIGGING.

I ACTUALLY SAW THE WHOLE THING IN PERSON. BUT MY POSITION WAS FAR FROM THE FIGHTING.

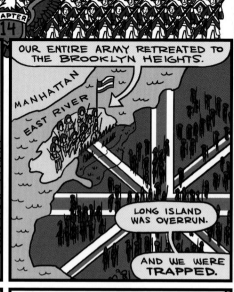

OUR ENTIRE ARMY RETREATED TO THE BROOKLYN HEIGHTS.

MANHATTAN

EAST RIVER

LONG ISLAND WAS OVERRUN.

AND WE WERE TRAPPED.

A DECISIVE VICTORY.

WON BY A PROFFESSIONAL FIGHTING FORCE.

NATE! I SEE YOU SURVIVED THE DAY!

I'M GLAD TO SEE YOU DID TOO!

THANKS TO THE MARYLAND BRIGADE. THEY SLOWED THE BRITISH SO WE COULD ESCAPE.

SPEAKING OF ESCAPE -- WASHINGTON IS SNEAKING EVERYONE OUT TONIGHT.

HOW'S HE GOING TO DO THAT?

CAN HE FLY?

JUST HAVE YOUR STUFF PACKED AND READY.

I'VE GOT EVERYTHING I OWN ON ME.

EVERYTHING I OWN IS SOAKED.

BE READY TO MOVE!

THAT WAS MYSTERIOUS.

THERE ARE THOUSANDS OF US. HOW CAN WASHINGTON SNEAK ALL OF US OUT?

CAN GEORGE WASHINGTON FLY?

NO, BUT HE CAN *PLAN.* REMEMBER, HE SET UP THE DORCHESTER HEIGHTS FORT IN ONE NIGHT.

YOU'LL SEE.

FOLLOW ME.

PSSSST COME THIS WAY, MEN. QUICKLY AND QUIETLY!

WHERE ARE WE GOING?

I DON'T BELIEVE IT! HE'S MOVING THE WHOLE ARMY ACROSS THE RIVER!?

SSSHH!

BE QUIET! IF WE'RE LUCKY, WE'LL GET **SOME** OF THE ARMY ACROSS.

THEN WE'LL WAIT. LET THE OTHERS GO AHEAD OF US-- ESPECIALLY THE WOUNDED.

THE WOUNDED ARE ALREADY ACROSS! FALL IN WITH THE REST, SOLDIER!

WHAT DO YOU MEAN **STUCK?**

THIS IS **ANNABELLE** --ONE OF MY BEST 12-POUNDERS!

ONE MORE PUSH! I DON'T LEAVE GUNS BEHIND!

NEED SOME HELP, OX?

HELLO, CAPTAIN HALE! GIVE US A HAND!

I'M ALWAYS MOVING THESE GUNS-- SOME DAY I'D LIKE TO SPEND TIME **SHOOTING** THEM.

WHAT ELSE CAN WE DO TO HELP?

AA-CHOoo!

GET ON THAT BOAT AND KEEP YOUR MOUTH SHUT! THAT'LL HELP!

THOSE ARE *ORDERS!*

AA-CHOoo!

YES, SIR.

THIS BOAT IS LOADED. ROW FOR IT.

PACKED IN LIKE PEAS IN A POD!

ARE YOU *SURE* WE WON'T SINK?

I'VE FERRIED TEN LOADS SO FAR-- HAVEN'T SUNK YET!

WON'T THE BRITS BE SURPRISED WHEN THEY FIND OUT WE'VE ALL ESCAPED!

ACHOOO!

I JUST HOPE WE CAN GET *EVERYBODY* ACROSS BEFORE MORNIN'!

IT'D BE A MIRACLE.

KEEP THE CAMPFIRES GOING! WE WANT THE BRITS TO THINK WE ARE ALL STILL CAMPED HERE IN BROOKLYN.

THEY'LL FIND OUT PRETTY QUICK WHEN THE SUN COMES UP.

THEN, IF WE'RE STILL HERE, WE'LL HAVE TO *FIGHT* FOR IT!

WHEN THE BRITISH FIGURE OUT WHAT'S GOING ON, THEY'LL STORM THIS POSITION.

IF THEY CAN SEE US. IT'S GETTING FOGGY.

YOUR TURN TO CROSS, BOYS. BETTER HURRY WHILE THIS FOG HOLDS.

SQUEEZE IN! WE'VE ONLY GOT A FEW BOATLOADS LEFT.

THIS IS SOME THICK FOG.

THIS IS SOME LUCKY FOG!

I CAN'T BELIEVE IT! THE WHOLE ARMY GOT ACROSS!

HEY, BEN!

SOME ESCAPE, HUH?

THANKS TO THE FOG!

SORRY ABOUT YOUR HORSE.

MY HORSE!!?

I FORGOT MY HORSE! I'VE GOT TO CROSS BACK AND GET HER!

I'VE HAD HER SINCE YALE! I'M GOING BACK!

FOR A HORSE!?

SEE YOU LATER! I'VE GOT TO GO SAVE MY HORSE!

YOU SURE ABOUT THIS?

SURE AS SURE.

WASHINGTON SNEAKED THE ENTIRE ARMY, ARTILLERY AND ALL, OFF OF LONG ISLAND. NOT A SINGLE LIFE WAS LOST.

OH GOOD.

AND BEN TALLMADGE RESCUED HIS HORSE.

SORRY, SWEETIE.

WHEN THE FOG CLEARED, THE BRITISH REALIZED THAT GEORGE WASHINGTON HAD TRICKED THEM ONCE AGAIN!

COR BLIMEY! THE YANKS 'AVE FLOWN THE COOP, THEY 'AVE!

HA-HA! YOU GAVE 'EM THE SLIP!

BIG DEAL. NOBODY EVER WON A WAR BY SNEAKING AWAY FROM THE FIGHT!

BUT WE WERE FREE TO FIGHT ANOTHER DAY. WASHINGTON'S ARMY WAS NOW ON MANHATTAN ISLAND.

CHAPTER 15

THE BRITISH ARE CLOSING IN. THEY'VE TAKEN OVER ALL OF LONG ISLAND.

OUR FORTIFICATIONS BARELY SLOWED THEM DOWN.

I CALL ON CAPTAIN HALE TO REPORT ON THE TROOP MOVEMENT AT THE BATTLE.

HE'S SICK, SIR. GOT A FEVER.

NOT YELLOW FEVER, I HOPE!

NO, SIR, JUST A REGULAR FEVER.

I HOPE HE GETS BETTER SOON.

IN ANY CASE, WE LOST 1,200 MEN. ALL WE HAVE LEFT IS THIS ISLAND, MANHATTAN.

CAN WE HOLD IT?

WE'RE OUTNUMBERED ON LAND AND SEA-- THEY CONTROL THE BAY. THEY COULD TAKE MANHATTAN IN ONE ATTACK.

AND THEY COULD ATTACK FROM ANYWHERE!

IF WE KNEW WHERE AND WHEN THEY PLANNED TO ATTACK, WE COULD STOP THEM.

I PROPOSE AN UNDERCOVER MISSION--

--A SPY MISSION.

SPYING IS FOR LOW-LIFE **SCUM**, NOT FOR PROPER SOLDIERS!

HEAR HIM! HEAR HIM!

WE'RE **RANGERS**, *NOT* **SPIES**!

SLAM

WE ARE FACING TWO-TO-ONE ODDS. THE FUTURE OF OUR COUNTRY DEPENDS ON THE INTELLIGENCE WE CAN DISCOVER!

SPYING IS THE **ONLY** WAY TO KNOW THEIR PLANS!

JAMES SPRAGUE, STEP FORWARD.

YES, SIR.

JAMES AND I FOUGHT IN THE FRENCH AND INDIAN WAR. HE'S AS CLEVER A SOLDIER AS I'VE EVER MET.

I WON'T **ORDER** YOU TO DO IT, JAMES, BUT I'LL **ASK** YOU...

WILL YOU BE OUR **SPY**?

SIR, I CAN'T DO IT.

CAN'T OR WON'T?

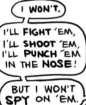

I **WON'T**. I'LL **FIGHT** 'EM, I'LL **SHOOT** 'EM, I'LL **PUNCH** 'EM IN THE **NOSE**!

BUT I WON'T **SPY** ON 'EM.

WHY NOT?

SPYIN'S JUST NO GOOD. THEY'LL CATCH ME AND STRING ME UP. THEY'LL HANG ME LIKE A DOG.

I WON'T DO IT.

ANYONE ELSE?

ANYONE?

CREAK

I'LL DO IT. I'LL BE YOUR SPY.

DON'T DO IT! SIR, DON'T GO!

IT'S A **SUICIDE** MISSION!

DO YOU KNOW ANY BETTER WAY TO GET THEIR PLANS?

WELL, *NO.* BUT NOT *YOU,* SIR. DON'T **DO** IT!

I OWE IT TO MY COUNTRY.

A-CHOO!

YOU'RE TOO **SICK,** SIR!

I HAVEN'T DONE ANYTHING IMPORTANT FOR OUR CAUSE.

COLONEL, IS THIS MISSION IMPORTANT?

MANHATTAN IS THE KEY TO THE CONTINENT. STOPPING THE BRITISH INVASION IS OUR **MOST** IMPORTANT MISSION.

LOOK AT HIS FACE.

HE'S TOO HONEST TO SPY!

I'M NOT ASHAMED TO SNEAK AND SPY FOR MY COUNTRY.

DON'T DO IT, NATE.

JUST **DON'T.**

I'M **GOING.** I'VE MADE UP MY MIND.

I'M THE SPY.

BOY, I BET YOU WISH YOU COULD TAKE **THAT** BACK.

NO. I'D DO IT AGAIN. IT WAS MY *DUTY.*

YOU ARE A BRAVE SOUL, MR. HALE.

STUPID, BUT **BRAVE.**

YOU WILL NEED A DISGUISE.

WHAT WILL YOUR COVER BE?

I'LL BE A DUTCH SCHOOLTEACHER, LOOKING FOR WORK

CAN YOU FIND SOME DUTCH CLOTHES?

YES, SIR. AND I HAVE MY DIPLOMA.

A PRIVATEER WILL TAKE YOU BACK TO LONG ISLAND.

CON-NECTICUT

LONG ISLAND

YOU WILL WALK THE ROADS, TAKING NOTES.

GET A TROOP COUNT AND A CAMP MAP.

TAKE **FOUR** DAYS. WALK TO **BROOKLYN**, THEN COME BACK. WE'LL PICK YOU UP.

I CAN DO THAT.

WE HAVE ONE MORE STOP BEFORE YOU GO.

WHERE?

YOU'LL SEE.

COLONEL KNOWLTON AND CAPTAIN HALE HERE TO SEE THE GENERAL.

ONE MOMENT, SIR.

HEY, CAPTAIN HALE!

KNOX THE OX!

I'VE JUST BEEN MADE **CHIEF OF ARTILLERY** FOR THE WHOLE **ARMY**.

WOW! THAT'S PERFECT!

JUST THINK; ALL THOSE GUNS AND I'M IN CHARGE OF THEM!

RIGHT THIS WAY, COLONEL.

YOU'LL DO GREAT, HENRY! BEST OF LUCK TO YOU!

WHICH GENERAL ARE WE MEETING? GREENE? PUTNAM?

AH, COLONEL KNOWLTON, WELCOME.

GENERAL WASHINGTON, THIS IS CAPTAIN HALE. HE'LL BE OUR MAN ON LONG ISLAND.

IT WILL BE MY HONOR TO SERVE, SIR.

A CAPTAIN GOING UNDERCOVER AS A SPY. YOU ARE VERY BRAVE.

THANK YOU, SIR.

SIT DOWN, I'M HAVING A QUICK SUPPER. JOIN ME.

WE'RE SENDING YOU RIGHT THROUGH THE ENEMY'S BACK DOOR.

YES, SIR.

HERE ARE THE CAMP LOCATIONS I SUSPECT.

OH, AND THIS IS FOR YOU.

WHAT IS IT?

THIS PAPER WILL GET YOU PASSAGE ON ANY AMERICAN SHIP.

SHOW IT TO THE CAPTAIN AND HE'LL TAKE YOU WHEREVER YOU NEED TO GO.

THANK YOU, SIR.

KEEP IT SAFE. IT COULD GET YOU OUT OF A JAM.

AFTER DINNER, I STARTED THE JOURNEY TO THE CROSSING POINT.

MY SPY ADVENTURE HAD BEGUN.

CHAPTER 16

SIR! SIR!

WAIT FOR ME!

YOU CAN'T COME WITH ME, SARGE.

WHY NOT?

I'M SUPPOSED TO BE A **TEACHER.** TEACHERS DON'T TRAVEL WITH **SERGEANTS.**

I'LL BE UNDERCOVER TOO! I'LL BE A... A...**BUTCHER!**

WHY WOULD A TEACHER TRAVEL WITH A BUTCHER?

FOR COMPANY?

COME WITH ME TO CONNECTICUT. BUT I CAN'T LET YOU CROSS THE WATER.

AFTER THAT, I GO **ALONE.**

OKAY.

IT'S GOOD TO SEE CONNECTICUT AGAIN.

HOME, SWEET HOME.

THAT COW LOOKS LIKE MY MIRACLE COW. REMEMBER THAT?

SURE DO.

HOW COULD I FORGET?

"BOOM!"

"KA-SPLAM!"

HA-HA!

POOR OLD MIRACLE COW.

THIS IS THE CROSSING POINT.

WE'RE LOOKING FOR A PRIVATEER CALLED THE SCHUYLER.

IS THAT CAPTAIN HALE I SEE?

AIN'T YOU SUPPOSED TO BE DEFENDING MANHATTAN?

HUH?

PONDY? IS THAT YOU?

IT'S OLD CAP'N POND!

HAVEN'T SEEN YOU TWO SINCE THE SIEGE OF BOSTON!

COME ABOARD!

JUST DON'T CHOP UP MY CARDS.

SO THEY PUT YOU ON THE WATER, HUH?

YUP. SURE BEATS THE ARMY!

WE'VE BEEN CATCHING BRITISH SHIPS AND CAUSING ALL KINDS OF TROUBLE.

SLAP

YOU OLD PIRATE!

PIRATE? THAT'S A DIRTY WORD! I'M A LEGAL PRIVATEER!

I RAID FOR MY COUNTRY!

DON'T FEEL BAD, PIRATE, I'M A SPY.

YOU ARE THE SPY?

I'M SUPPOSED TO TAKE YOU ACROSS THE SOUND!

THIS SHIP IS THE SCHUYLER?

SURE IS!

I'LL TAKE YOU ACROSS TONIGHT.

UNDER COVER OF DARKNESS.

90

YOU AREN'T PLANNING ON SPYING IN SOLDIER'S CLOTHES, ARE YOU?

OF COURSE NOT! HE'LL BE DRESSED UP AS A DUTCH SCHOOLTEACHER.

THAT SHOULD BE EASY. YOU *ARE* A SCHOOLTEACHER.

HOW DO I LOOK?

LIKE A SOLDIER DISGUISED AS A SCHOOLTEACHER.

YOU LOOK LIKE A TEACHER TO ME.

NOT QUITE YET.

A POOR TEACHER WOULDN'T HAVE SILVER BUCKLES.

HERE, TAKE THESE.

I'LL KEEP 'EM POLISHED FOR YOU.

AND HERE ARE MY PAPERS.

YOU NEVER GOT TO USE YOUR WASHINGTON SHIP PASS.

WHAT'S THAT?

WOW! YOU COULD ORDER ME TO CUBA WITH THIS AND I'D HAVE TO TAKE YOU THERE.

LET'S DO *THAT!* LET'S SAIL TO *CUBA!*

YOU KNOW I CAN'T DO THAT, SARGE.

I'M READY.

TAKE ME ACROSS.

KEEP YOUR EYES PEELED...

...THESE WATERS ARE PATROLLED BY BRITISH *HUNTER-KILLER* SHIPS.

EEE. *HUNTER-KILLERS?*

I DON'T LIKE THE SOUND OF THOSE.

THERE ARE MORE OF THEM EVERY DAY.

CAPTAIN, WE'VE SPOTTED THE H.M.S. *HALIFAX*.

THAT'S *TROUBLE!*

SHE'S A HUNTER-KILLER!

CAPTAIN HALE, WE'RE GOING TO HAVE TO SEND YOU IN BY ROWBOAT.

WE CAN'T TANGLE WITH THE *HALIFAX*.

CAPTAIN, THERE'S A REBEL SHIP IN THE SOUND.

A BIG ONE?

NO, IT'S THE SCHUYLER.

THAT PESKY LITTLE PIRATE!

SHOULD WE MAKE CHASE, SIR?

NO, THEY ARE TURNING BACK.

KEEP YOURSELF **SAFE** OVER THERE, NATE.

ARE YOU SURE I CAN'T COME ALONG?

NOT THIS TIME, SARGE.

GOOD LUCK, MY FRIEND.

I HOPE MY LUCK HOLDS.

IT DIDN'T.

I WAS SPOTTED THE **SECOND** I SET FOOT ON LONG ISLAND.

WHO'S **THAT** GUY?

HE'S CREEPY.

THAT IS MAJOR ROBERT ROGERS.

HA! YOU WERE SPOTTED BY **MAJOR ROGERS**-- OF ROGERS' RANGERS?

IT'S OFFICIAL, YOU TRULY ARE THE WORLD'S **UNLUCKIEST SPY.**

WHO'S MAJOR ROGERS?

OH, HE'S THE **DEVIL HIMSELF.**

YOU GOT CAUGHT BY THE **DEVIL HIMSELF?**

MAJOR ROBERT ROGERS... HOW SHOULD I DESCRIBE HIM?

CHAPTER 17

HE'S A LOT LIKE YOUR MAN THOMAS KNOWLTON.

IF KNOWLTON WAS **PURE EVIL.**

ROBERT ROGERS ALSO FOUGHT IN THE FRENCH AND INDIAN WAR.

HE WAS KNOWN FOR **SCALPING** ENEMIES.

AFTER THAT WAR, HE WENT TO ENGLAND,

WHERE HIS SCHEMES PUT HIM IN PRISON FOR THREE YEARS.

WHEN THIS WAR STARTED, HE CAME HOME TO BE A SPY.

A SPY FOR WHICH SIDE?

WHICHEVER SIDE PAID THE MOST.

HE WANTED TO BE A **DOUBLE AGENT**...

...SPYING FOR **BOTH** SIDES—AND GETTING **PAID** BY BOTH SIDES.

YOU'VE GOT TO BE A **SNEAKY DEVIL** TO MAKE THAT TRICK WORK.

AMERICAN SECRETS

BRITISH SECRETS

HE WAS.

HIS PLAN DIDN'T LAST, THOUGH. WASHINGTON CAPTURED HIM.

LOCK UP THIS VILLAIN!

HE ESCAPED...

...MADE HIS WAY TO THE HARBOR...

...SWAM OUT TO THE BRITISH FLAGSHIP...

...CLIMBED UP THE ANCHOR CHAIN...

AND POPPED INTO ADMIRAL HOWE'S DINNER PARTY.

THE ADMIRAL WAS SO IMPRESSED, HE INVITED HIM TO DINNER AND GAVE HIM HIS OWN RANGER UNIT.

SMASHING!

GOOD SHOW!

BRAVO!

SO WHEN YOU STEPPED OUT OF THAT ROWBOAT, YOU WERE SPOTTED BY THE **MOST DANGEROUS MAN** ON LONG ISLAND.

YEAH. PRETTY MUCH.

WHAT HAPPENED? DID HE RUN UP AND CATCH YOU?

NO, HE WAS MORE CLEVER THAN THAT.

HE SENT HIS MEN TO FOLLOW ME.

DID YOU KNOW YOU'D BEEN SPOTTED?

NO.

I THOUGHT I'D MADE A SECRET LANDING.

I SET OUT ON MY SPY MISSION.

HELLO, SIR, I AM A TEACHER LOOKING FOR WORK.

MAY I SLEEP IN YOUR BARN?

SURE YE CAN.

AIN'T NO SCHOOLS ROUND HERE, THOUGH.

I MADE MY WAY TO BROOKLYN, TAKING NOTES ON EVERYTHING I SAW.

AND EVERY STEP WAS WATCHED BY ROGERS.

MEANWHILE, BACK IN MANHATTAN, BRITISH AND HESSIAN TROOPS HAD STARTED THEIR INVASION.

THE CONTINENTAL ARMY WAS PUSHED TO THE NORTH END OF MANHATTAN, TO THE **HARLEM HEIGHTS**.

MANHATTAN

LONG ISLAND

WARSHIPS MOVED IN AND BEGAN POUNDING THE HARBOR FORTS.

THE AMERICANS WERE LOSING HEART.

AND LOSING THE WAR! THEY'D GIVEN UP-- WE CAPTURED THEM BY THE *HUNDREDS!*

WHAT DO YOU DO WITH ALL OF THE PRISONERS?

HANG THEM?

GOOD HEAVENS, NO! WE DO NOT KILL PRISONERS OF WAR!

THAT WOULD BE **BARBARIC!**

SADLY, HANGING WOULD BE KINDER FOR MANY OF THE PRISONERS.

WHAT DO YOU MEAN?

THOUSANDS OF AMERICANS ARE PUT INTO PRISON SHIPS.

THEY SPEND MONTHS CHAINED, FLOATING IN NEW YORK HARBOR.

MANY DIE THERE FROM DISEASE AND STARVATION.

LIES! ALL LIES!

BEN TALLMADGE'S BROTHER DIES ON A PRISON SHIP.

HE **STARVES** TO DEATH.

UGH. I'D RATHER HANG WITH A FULL BELLY THAN STARVE TO DEATH SLOWLY, THAT'S FOR **SURE!**

THE INVASION OF NEW YORK WAS ALMOST COMPLETE.

AND THERE I WAS, TRYING TO FIGURE OUT WHEN IT WAS GOING TO **START**.

YOUR MISSION WAS NOW USELESS.

WAIT! I THOUGHT IT WAS SUPER-IMPORTANT!

IT WAS WHEN I STARTED. BUT THE WAR HAD MOVED ON WITHOUT ME.

WHAT DID YOU DO?

I TRIED TO MAKE THE BEST OF IT.

I CAN STILL SPY OUT TROOP STRENGTH.

THERE IS STILL VALUABLE INFORMATION TO BRING BACK.

THERE'S ALWAYS NEWS IN A TAVERN. I'LL POP IN AND LISTEN TO THE GOSSIP.

INN

WHAT'S FOR DINNER?

WE'VE GOT SOME RABBIT STEW.

ANYONE SITTING HERE?

DON'T TRUST HIM!

NO, SIR--HAVE A SEAT.

THANKS.

WHAT'S YOUR STORY, FRIEND?

I'M A TEACHER. I'M LOOKING FOR WORK.

YOU TEACH LITTLE KIDDIES 'BOUT READIN' AND SUCH?

I DO.

MUST BE HARD, FINDIN' TEACHER WORK DURIN' WAR TIME.

IT IS HARD, YES.

HOW D'YA LIKE ALL THESE BRITISH SOLDIERS MOVIN' IN AND TAKIN' OVER?

UM. THEY ARE... GOOD.

I LIKE THEM.

YOU TRULY ARE THE WORST SPY IN HISTORY.

I'LL TELL YA A SECRET, FRIEND, I DON'T LIKE 'EM. NOT ONE BIT.

YOU DON'T?

NOPE. I THINK GEORGE WASHIN'TON OUGHT TO KICK 'EM ALL OUT.

OH YEAH?

ME AN' SOME FRIENDS ARE WORKIN' AGAINST 'EM FROM THE INSIDE.

WE'RE SPIES.

DON'T SAY ANYTHING!

I'M A SPY TOO!

I'VE BEEN SENT TO GATHER INTELLIGENCE-- BY GENERAL WASHINGTON HIMSELF.

YOU DON'T **SAY!**

WE COULD WORK *TOGETHER!*

WE COULD!

CAN MY FRIENDS HELP OUT TOO? THEY SURE WOULD LOVE TO.

YES! THE MORE THE BETTER!

BUT NOT NOW...

WE NEED TO ARRANGE A **SECRET** TIME **LATER**, TO MAKE SURE IT IS **SAFE.**

GOOD THINKING!

YOU HAVE TO THINK LIKE A SPY, IF YOU DON'T WANNA GET CAUGHT.

THE ENEMY IS EVERY- WHERE.

CHAPTER 18

THE ENEMY IS EVERYWHERE!

THAT LOOKS LIKE THE 42ND REGIMENT--THE **BLACK WATCH.** ALONG WITH ABOUT **400** HESSIANS.

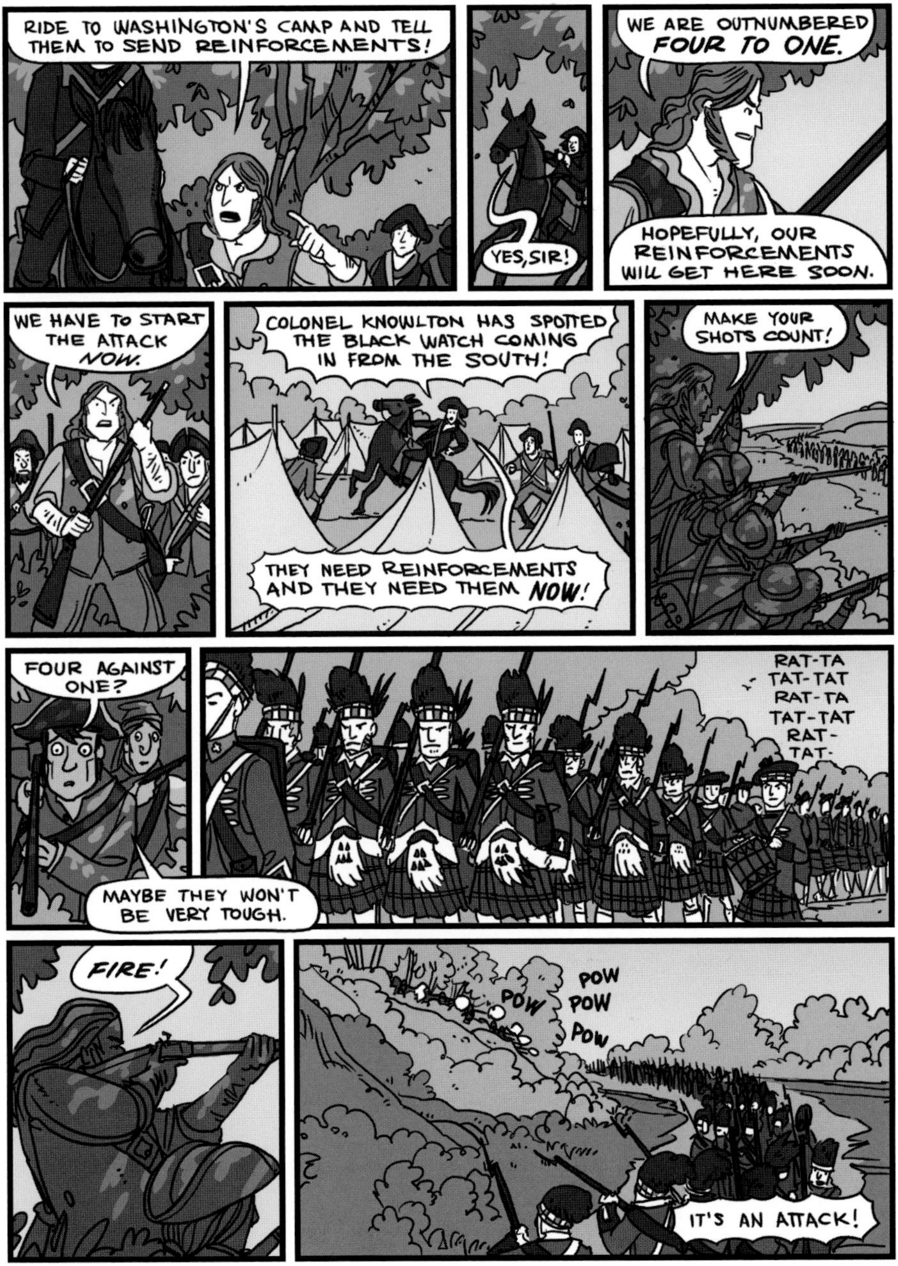
RIDE TO WASHINGTON'S CAMP AND TELL THEM TO SEND REINFORCEMENTS!
YES, SIR!
WE ARE OUTNUMBERED FOUR TO ONE.
HOPEFULLY, OUR REINFORCEMENTS WILL GET HERE SOON.
WE HAVE TO START THE ATTACK NOW.
COLONEL KNOWLTON HAS SPOTTED THE BLACK WATCH COMING IN FROM THE SOUTH!
THEY NEED REINFORCEMENTS AND THEY NEED THEM NOW!
MAKE YOUR SHOTS COUNT!
FOUR AGAINST ONE?
MAYBE THEY WON'T BE VERY TOUGH.
RAT-TA TAT-TAT RAT-TA TAT-TAT RAT-TAT-
FIRE!
POW POW POW POW
IT'S AN ATTACK!

POW POW

THAT'S THE RANGERS! THEY'VE STARTED THE ATTACK ALREADY!

RUN!

ON THE DOUBLE! WE'VE GOT TO HELP!

HOLD YOUR GROUND AND KEEP *FIRING*!

CLICK

COLONEL, THE REINFORCEMENTS ARE CLOSE!

EXCELLENT!

FALL BACK, MEN! GET THEM TO **CHASE US**!

THE COWARDS ARE *RUNNIN'*!

CRACK

BANG

AFTER 'EM, LADDIES!

TOOOOT

TALLYHO! HA-HA! JUST LIKE A FOX HUNT!

GIVE UP, YA WEE FOXES!

THEY FELL FOR OUR TRAP!

!?!

FIRE!

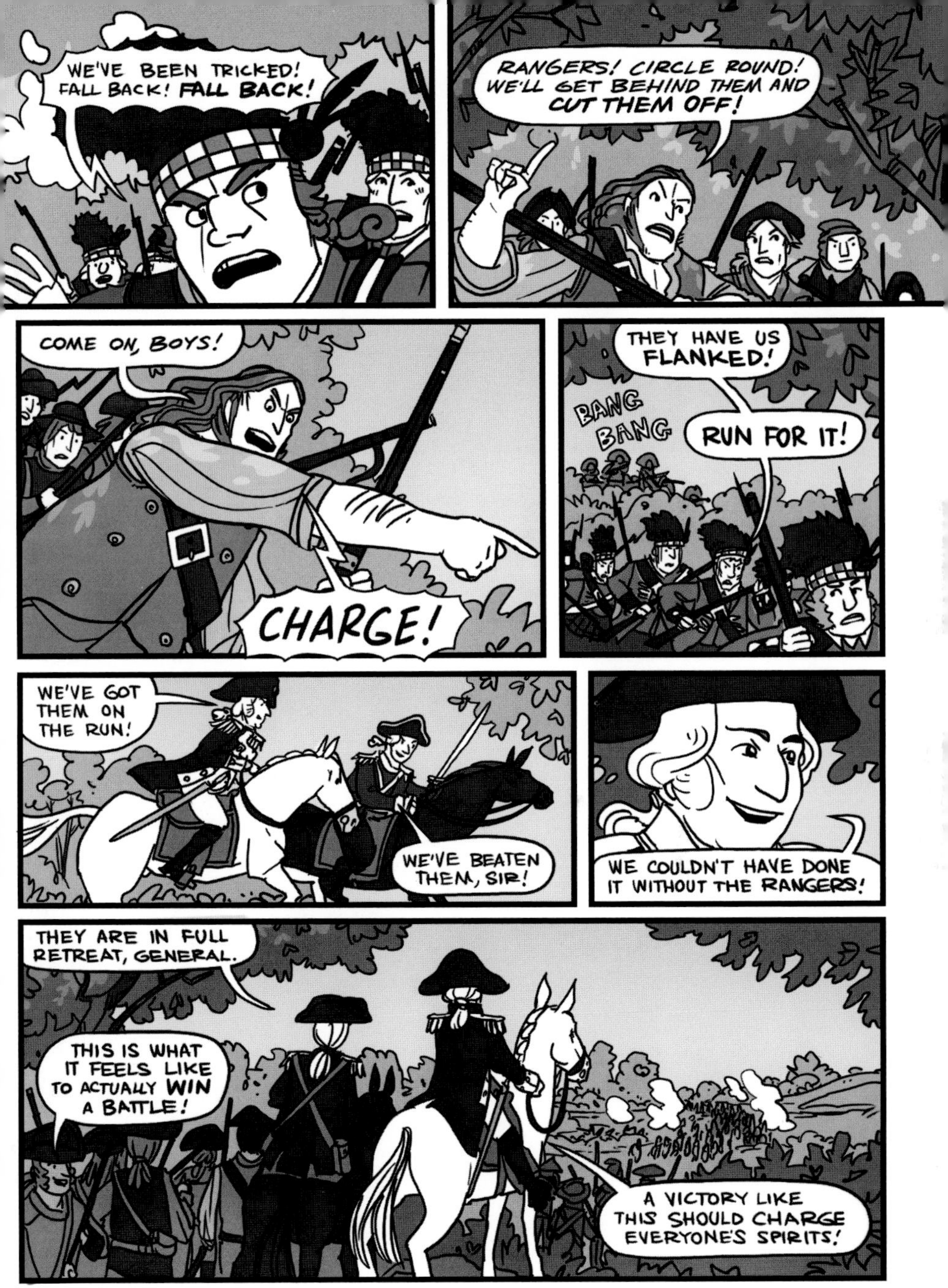
WE'VE BEEN TRICKED! FALL BACK! FALL BACK!
RANGERS! CIRCLE ROUND! WE'LL GET BEHIND THEM AND CUT THEM OFF!
COME ON, BOYS!
CHARGE!
THEY HAVE US FLANKED!
BANG BANG
RUN FOR IT!
WE'VE GOT THEM ON THE RUN!
WE'VE BEATEN THEM, SIR!
WE COULDN'T HAVE DONE IT WITHOUT THE RANGERS!
THEY ARE IN FULL RETREAT, GENERAL.
THIS IS WHAT IT FEELS LIKE TO ACTUALLY WIN A BATTLE!
A VICTORY LIKE THIS SHOULD CHARGE EVERYONE'S SPIRITS!

WHERE IS COLONEL KNOWLTON?

HE DIDN'T MAKE IT, SIR.

WHAT!?

BUT HE WAS A **HERO**!

HE WAS A HERO. AND HE DIED LEADING HIS MEN IN A CHARGE THAT DAY ON THE HARLEM HEIGHTS.

WHY ARE YOU TELLING US SUCH **SAD** STORIES.?

IT GETS SADDER.

IT **DOES**?

YES, BUT THEN IT GETS HAPPIER.

IT **DOES**?

WELL, HAPPY FOR US-- THE **AMERICANS**--NOT FOR YOUR SIDE.

I DOUBT THAT.

JUST YOU WAIT. THIS WAR WILL **KNOCK** YOUR **SOCKS** OFF!

IT WILL? DOES THE WAR END SOON?

OH NO, THIS WAR HAS ONLY JUST BEGUN. I'LL HAVE TO TELL YOU HOW IT ENDS ANOTHER TIME.

ANOTHER TIME? YOU DON'T **HAVE** ANOTHER TIME. WE'RE ABOUT TO **HANG** YOU.

TRUE. BUT I'M WILLING TO BET YOU WILL WANT TO HEAR MORE.

WAIT, **WAIT!** YOU HAVEN'T TOLD US THE END OF YOUR **OWN** STORY YET!

CHAPTER 19

I WENT TO MEET HIM AT THE SECRET MEETING PLACE.

HOW DID ROGERS CATCH YOU?

INN

THAT LOOKS LIKE THE SAME INN.

IT WAS, BUT IT WAS AT A **SECRET TIME.**

ROGERS HAD FILLED THE TAVERN WITH HIS MEN. IT WAS A **TRAP.**

PSST. HERE HE IS BOYS, WASHIN'TON'S TOP SPY.

IS THAT TRUE?

YES, IT IS.

HE ADMITS IT! YOU ARE ALL WITNESSES!

CATCH THE SPY!

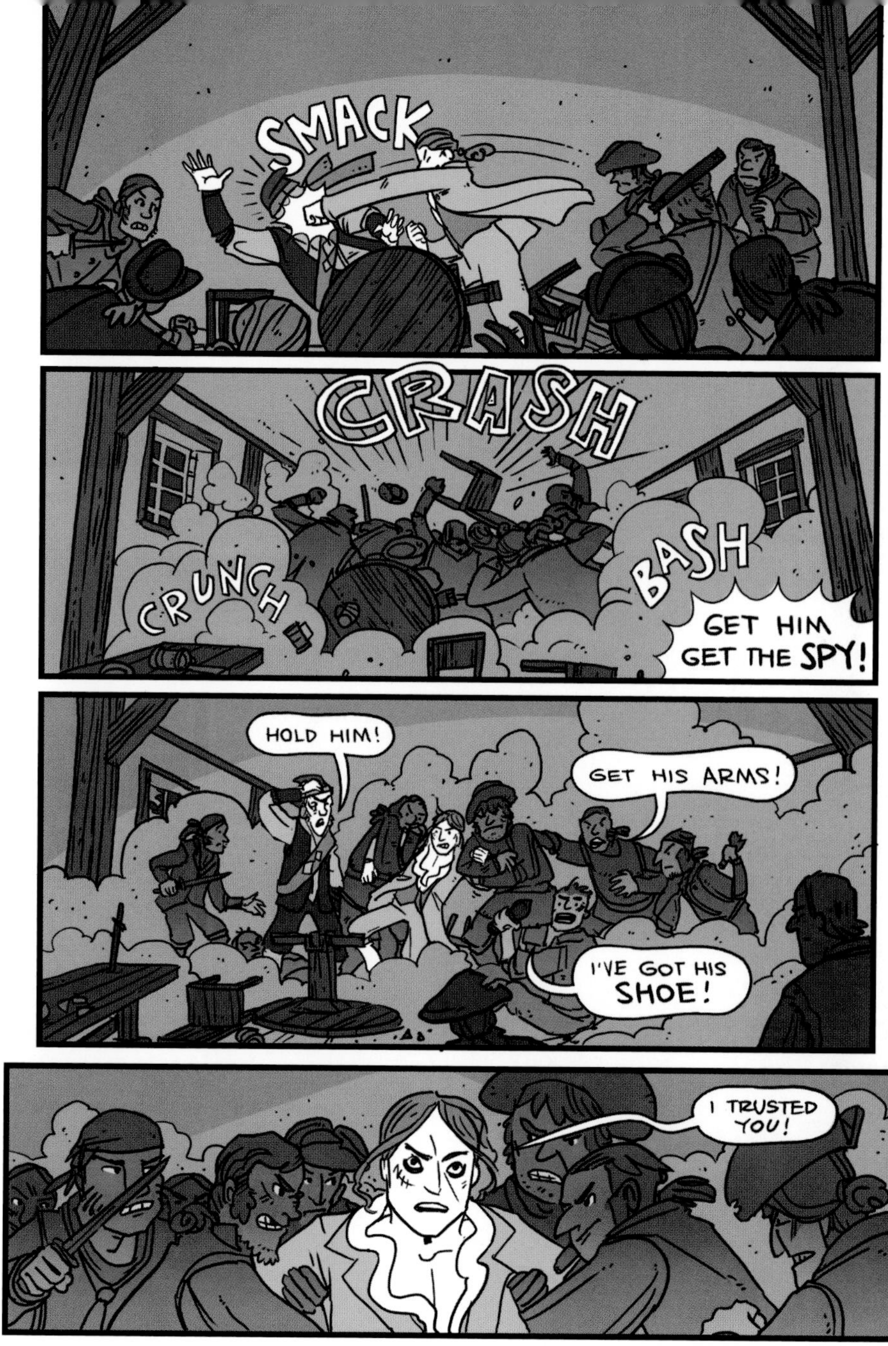
SMACK
CRASH
CRUNCH
BASH
GET HIM GET THE SPY!
HOLD HIM!
GET HIS ARMS!
I'VE GOT HIS SHOE!
I TRUSTED YOU!

ONE MISTAKE OF **MANY**, BOY-O!

I FOUND THESE IN HIS SHOE!

TSK TSK. I HOPE THESE AREN'T DRAWIN'S OF BRITISH TROOPS AND POSITIONS.

THEY **ARE!** THIS IS BAD NEWS FOR YOU, SPY. DRAWIN'S ARE NICE, THOUGH.

YOU SHOULD HAVE BEEN AN ARTIST, NOT A SPY.

GENERAL HOWE WILL BE **VERY** INTERESTED IN THESE.

YOU'RE TAKING ME TO GENERAL **HOWE**?

YES, YOU WILL BE MY LITTLE PRESENT FOR HIM.

I'M TAKING YOU TO HIM PERSONALLY, ON MY OWN SHIP.

HE DID.

DID YOU MEET GENERAL HOWE?

I DID.

* COUGH *
* COUGH *

I WENT FROM GENERAL WASHINGTON TO GENERAL HOWE IN JUST A FEW DAYS.

THERE IS A FIRE DESTROYING NEW YORK. DID YOU START THAT FIRE?

NO, I DID NOT LIGHT THE FIRE.

IT'S BLASTED INCONVENIENT! JUST AS WE CAPTURE NEW YORK, SOME FOOL REBEL **BURNS IT DOWN**!

YOU MUST KNOW BY NOW THAT YOUR ARMY HAS BEEN DEFEATED.

WE NOW CONTROL LONG ISLAND **AND** MANHATTAN.

IT IS A PAINFUL DEFEAT. BUT I LIT NO FIRES.

HMM. I BELIEVE YOU.

YOU DON'T ACTUALLY SEEM CAPABLE OF LYING.

I IMAGINE THAT IS WHY I WAS SO EASY TO CATCH.

SO YOU ADMIT TO BEING A SPY.

WHAT DO YOU HAVE TO SAY FOR YOURSELF.

I AM **NATHAN HALE** FROM CONNECTICUT. I AM A CAPTAIN IN **KNOWLTON'S RANGERS**. I WAS SENT BY GENERAL WASHINGTON TO SPY OUT PLANS FOR THE BRITISH INVASION OF NEW YORK.

YOU ARE A BRAVE MAN, CAPTAIN HALE.

I ONLY WISH I COULD HAVE SERVED MY COUNTRY BETTER.

AS IS THE RULE IN WAR, YOU WILL BE HANGED.

TOMORROW MORNING. I WON'T MAKE YOU WAIT.

ANY LAST REQUESTS?

MAY I HAVE A BIBLE TO READ AND A CHAPLAIN AT THE HANGING?

NO, YOU MAY NOT.

TAKE HIM AWAY.

I SPENT THE NIGHT LOCKED IN A GREENHOUSE.

A GREENHOUSE? THAT'S AN ODD JAIL.

THERE WASN'T TIME TO PUT ME ON A PRISON SHIP.

IN THE MORNING I WAS MARCHED TO THE GALLOWS.

HEY! I KNOW THAT GUY!

I SAID MY LAST WORDS:

I REGRET THAT I HAVE BUT ONE LIFE TO GIVE FOR MY COUNTRY.

THEN THE GIANT BOOK ATE ME...

AND HERE WE ARE.

BUT WHAT ABOUT GEORGE WASHINGTON AND HENRY KNOX -- AND BEN TALLMADGE? WHERE ARE THEY? WHAT HAPPENED TO THEM?

THEY ARE RUNNING AWAY, IN **FULL RETREAT.**

IT'S TRUE. THE CONTINENTAL ARMY IS NOW RETREATING THROUGH NEW JERSEY.

WE NOW CONTROL NEW YORK, LONG ISLAND -- AND SOON THE **WHOLE** SILLY COUNTRY!

NOT QUITE. YOU HAVE SOME SURPRISES COMING.

WHAT? WHAT SURPRISES?

I WANT TO KNOW WHAT HAPPENS *NEXT!*

YOU *REALLY* WANT TO KNOW WHAT HAPPENS?

YES!! REALLY! REALLY! REALLY!

WE WIN.

WHAT?

WE WIN THE WAR. THE BRITISH GO HOME. AMERICA BECOMES ITS OWN COUNTRY.

ONE DAY AMERICA BECOMES THE MOST POWERFUL COUNTRY IN THE WORLD.

POPPY-COCK!

THERE IS *NO WAY* THAT YOUR DIRTY LITTLE ARMY CAN STAND AGAINST THE *FINEST ARMY* THE *WORLD HAS EVER KNOWN!*

IT *IS* A LITTLE UNBELIEVABLE. BUT THAT'S WHAT HAPPENS.

PANT PANT

PANT

HOW? HOW DO WE-- I MEAN *YOU*--WIN?

MORE BATTLES, MORE SPIES, MORE TRICKS BY WASHINGTON...

...THIS WAR HAS JUST STARTED.

THERE ARE MANY, *MANY, MANY* MORE EXCITING STORIES IN AMERICA'S BOOK OF HISTORY.

BUT I WANT TO KNOW *RIGHT NOW!*

SO DO I!

SO YOU WANT TO HEAR MORE STORIES?

YES!!

YOU DON'T MIND PUTTING OFF THE HANGING WHILE I TELL THEM?

WE'VE GOT TIME FOR A FEW MORE STORIES.

TELL THEM!

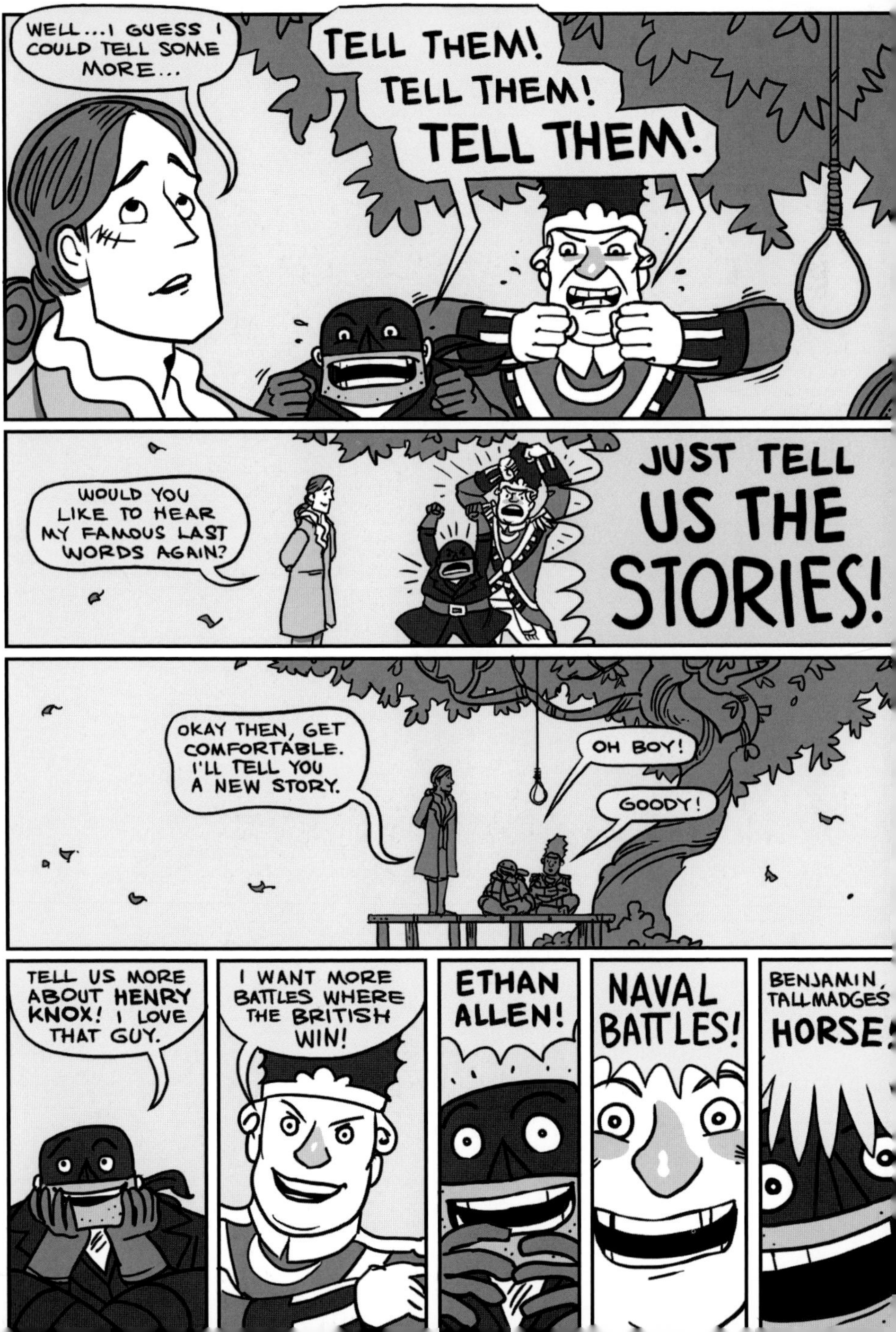
WELL...I GUESS I COULD TELL SOME MORE...
TELL THEM! TELL THEM! TELL THEM!
WOULD YOU LIKE TO HEAR MY FAMOUS LAST WORDS AGAIN?
JUST TELL US THE STORIES!
OKAY THEN, GET COMFORTABLE. I'LL TELL YOU A NEW STORY.
OH BOY!
GOODY!
TELL US MORE ABOUT HENRY KNOX! I LOVE THAT GUY.
I WANT MORE BATTLES WHERE THE BRITISH WIN!
ETHAN ALLEN!
NAVAL BATTLES!
BENJAMIN, TALLMADGE'S HORSE!

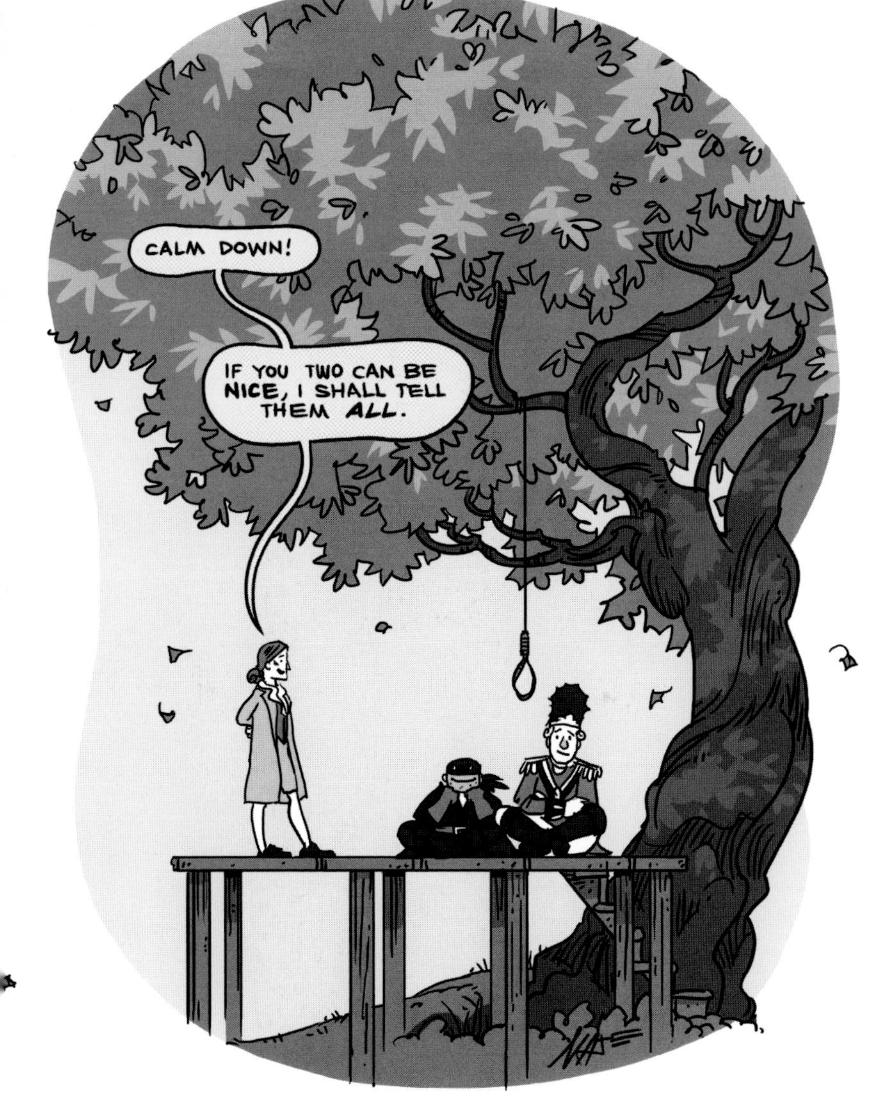
CALM DOWN!
IF YOU TWO CAN BE NICE, I SHALL TELL THEM ALL.

TO BE CONTINUED...

NH
HT

NATHAN HALE'S HAZARDOUS TALES

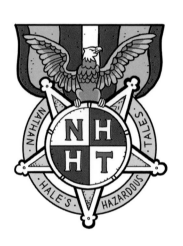

NATHAN HALE (JUNE 6, 1755 — SEPTEMBER 22, 1776)

AFTER A NIGHT AT THE TAVERN, NATHAN HALE AND HIS FRIENDS REALLY DID SMASH SEVERAL WINDOWS AT YALE COLLEGE. THE EXACT REASON WHY IS NOT KNOWN.

NATHAN HALE WAS EXECUTED IN 1776. HE WAS TWENTY-ONE YEARS OLD. HIS BODY WAS NEVER FOUND.

WOW! NICE STATUE!

THEY MAKE A FEW STATUES OF ME, AND NAME THINGS AFTER ME TOO, SCHOOLS, FORTS, EVEN A NAVY SUBMARINE.

HENRY KNOX
"KNOX THE OX"
(JULY 25, 1750 — OCTOBER 25, 1806)

HENRY KNOX WAS AT THE BOSTON MASSACRE-- HE EVEN TRIED TO STOP THE BRITISH FROM FIRING. HE WAS WASHINGTON'S YOUNGEST MAJOR GENERAL. HE EVENTUALLY BECAME THE SECRETARY OF WAR. MANY WANTED HIM TO BE THE FIRST *VICE PRESIDENT,* BUT HE PREFERRED THE ARMY.

HE DIED FROM INFECTION WHEN A CHICKEN BONE GOT STUCK IN HIS THROAT.

A CHICKEN BONE!?

THOMAS KNOWLTON
(NOVEMBER 22, 1740 - SEPTEMBER 16, 1776)

THOMAS KNOWLTON WAS ONE OF WASHINGTON'S FIRST SPYMASTERS (A JOB BENJAMIN TALLMADGE WOULD LATER HAVE). HE FORMED AMERICA'S FIRST SPECIAL FORCES UNIT, *KNOWLTON'S RANGERS.* THE SEAL OF THE ARMY INTELLIGENCE SERVICE HAS THE DATE "1776" ON IT. THIS DATE MARKS THE FORMATION OF KNOWLTON'S RANGERS.

THOMAS KNOWLTON DIED SIX DAYS BEFORE NATHAN HALE DID. HE HAD NINE CHILDREN.

ETHAN ALLEN (JANUARY 21, 1738 – FEB 12, 1789)

ACCORDING TO ETHAN ALLEN'S OWN RECORD OF THE CAPTURE OF FORT TICONDEROGA, HE CLAIMED TO HAVE SAID, "[COME OUT] IN THE NAME OF THE GREAT JEHOVAH AND THE CONTINENTAL CONGRESS!" WHICH ISN'T NEARLY AS CATCHY AS "COME OUT OF THERE, YOU DAMNED OLD RAT!"

AFTER HIS CAPTURE OF FORT TICONDEROGA WITH THE GREEN MOUNTAIN BOYS AND HIS FAILED RAID ON MONTREAL, ETHAN ALLEN WAS HELD PRISONER UNTIL 1778. DURING THAT TIME, HIS VARIOUS PRISON SHIPS TRAVELED FAR AND WIDE. HE WAS TAKEN FROM MONTREAL TO ENGLAND AND IRELAND, THEN TO NEW YORK. THEN HE WAS DROPPED OFF ON AN ICY SHORE IN HALIFAX.

AFTER HIS RELEASE, HE VISITED GEORGE WASHINGTON AT VALLEY FORGE. HE EVENTUALLY MOVED BACK TO VERMONT, THE STATE HE HELPED FORM.

BENEDICT ARNOLD (JANUARY, 14, 1741– ███████

BENEDICT ARNOLD WAS A TALENTED GENERAL WHO ███████ A ███████████████████ ████████████████████ AND ███████████████ THE ███████████ ████████████████ BEFORE BECOMING █████████████████ OF THE █████████████████ HELPED ███████████████! WHERE THEY BUILT A STATUE OF HIS LEG.

> HEY! WHY IS IT ALL BLACKED OUT! WHAT DID BENEDICT ARNOLD DO?

> I'M SAVING THAT STUFF FOR ANOTHER STORY. IT'S A JUICY STORY TOO.

ROBERT ROGERS (NOVEMBER 7, 1731 – MAY 18, 1795)

ROGERS' CAPTURE OF NATHAN HALE IS JUST A FOOT-NOTE IN HIS LONG AND STRANGE MILITARY CAREER.

WITH HIS RANGER UNIT, *ROGERS' RANGERS*, HE FOUGHT IN SOME OF THE FIERCEST BATTLES OF THE FRENCH AND INDIAN WAR. HIS SPECIALTY WAS OPERATING IN MOUNTAINS AND SNOW. HE ONCE ESCAPED A FRENCH AMBUSH BY SLIDING 400 FEET DOWN AN ICY ROCKFACE. THE FRENCH FOUND HIS REGIMENTAL COAT AND REPORTED HIM AS *KILLED IN ACTION*.

ROBERT ROGERS WROTE A GUIDEBOOK ON RANGERING, PUBLISHED A JOURNAL AND EVEN WROTE A PLAY THAT WAS PERFORMED IN ENGLAND.

IN 1940, SPENCER TRACY PLAYED HIM IN A MOVIE CALLED *NORTHWEST PASSAGE.*

> WHAT'S A *MOVIE?*

STEPHEN HEMPSTEAD (JUNE 6, 1754–OCTOBER 3, 1831)

SERGEANT STEPHEN HEMPSTEAD (CALLED "SARGE" IN THIS BOOK) WAS A FRIEND OF NATHAN HALE'S FROM YALE AND NEW LONDON, CONNECTICUT. THEY SHARED THE SAME BIRTHDAY.

AFTER SEEING HALE OFF ON HIS SPY MISSION, HEMPSTEAD RETURNED TO ACTIVE DUTY. HE FOUGHT IN THE BATTLE OF HARLEM HEIGHTS, WHERE HE WAS INJURED AND LEFT FOR DEAD ON THE BATTLEFIELD. IN SEPTEMBER OF 1781, HE WAS A DEFENDER AT FORT GRISWOLD. HE WAS CAPTURED BY THE BRITISH, STRIPPED NAKED, AND PUSHED DOWN A HILL IN AN AMMUNITION CART. IT TOOK HIM ELEVEN MONTHS TO RECOVER. HE HAD TO RECOVER AT HIS BROTHER'S HOUSE--THE BRITISH HAD BURNED HIS HOUSE DOWN.

BENJAMIN TALLMADGE (FEBRUARY 11, 1754–MARCH 7, 1835)

BEN TALLMADGE BECAME THE SPY NATHAN HALE ALWAYS WANTED TO BE. HE WAS WASHINGTON'S CHIEF INTELLIGENCE OFFICER. HE FORMED WASHINGTON'S SPY NETWORK, "THE CULPER RING."

THE EXECUTION OF NATHAN HALE IS SHROUDED IN MYSTERY. THERE ARE FEW EYEWITNESS ACCOUNTS AND THEY DON'T AGREE ON THE EVENTS OF THE ACTUAL HANGING OR THE LAST WORDS SPOKEN BY HALE. THERE ARE TWO DIFFERENT PLAQUES IN MANHATTAN CLAIMING TO BE THE LOCATION OF THE HANGING TREE. ONE OF THEM IS ON A **BANANA REPUBLIC** STORE (3RD AVENUE AND 65TH STREET.)

HALE WAS NOT EXECUTED ON A FORMAL GALLOWS (AS PORTRAYED IN THIS BOOK) RATHER, HE WAS FORCED TO JUMP FROM A LADDER, WITH A NOOSE AROUND HIS NECK.

HIS OFFICIAL REGIMENTAL RECORD READS SIMPLY: NATHAN HALE—CAPT—KILLED—22d SEPT.

117

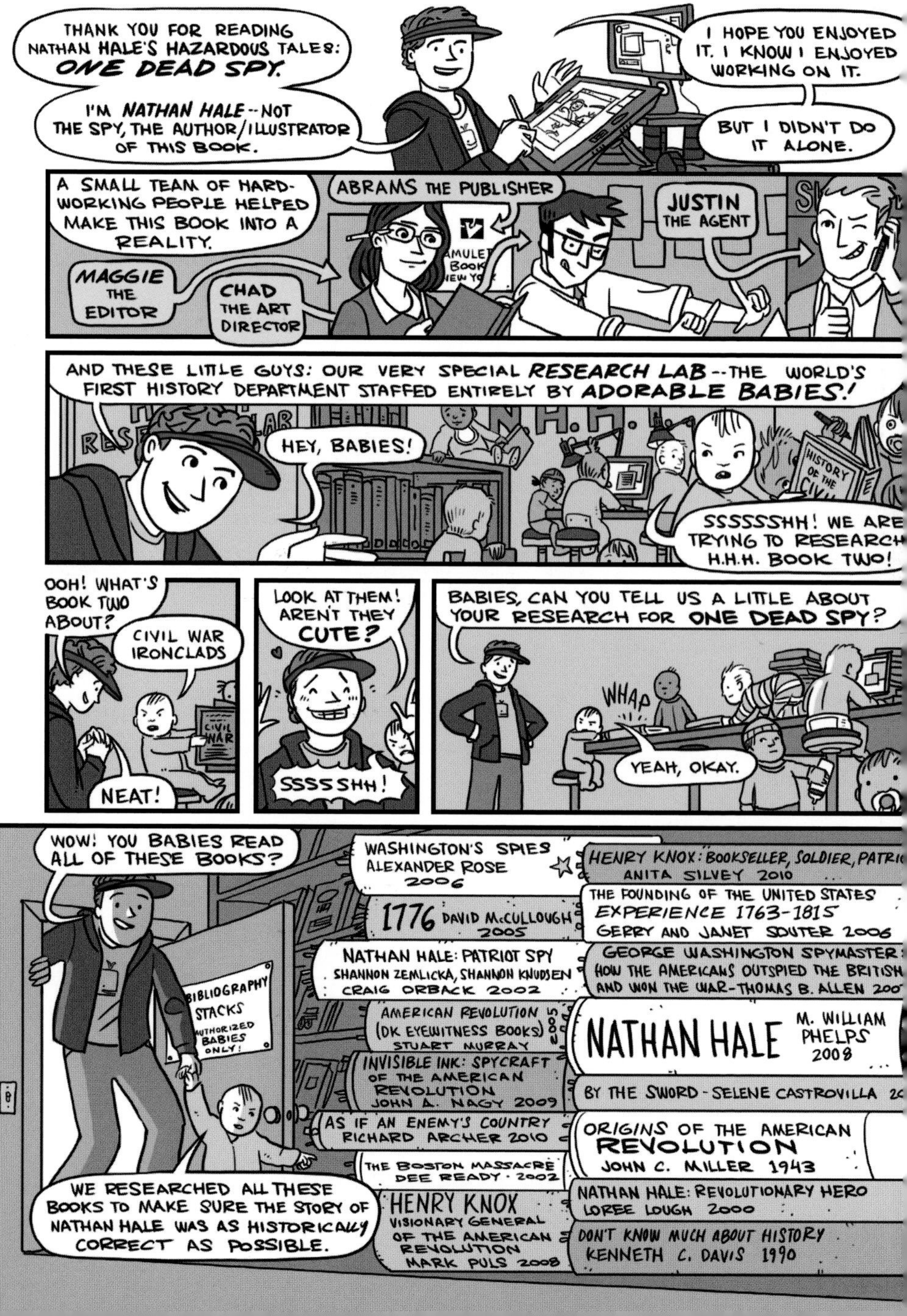
THANK YOU FOR READING NATHAN HALE'S HAZARDOUS TALES: *ONE DEAD SPY.*
I'M *NATHAN HALE*--NOT THE SPY, THE AUTHOR/ILLUSTRATOR OF THIS BOOK.
I HOPE YOU ENJOYED IT. I KNOW I ENJOYED WORKING ON IT.
BUT I DIDN'T DO IT ALONE.
A SMALL TEAM OF HARD-WORKING PEOPLE HELPED MAKE THIS BOOK INTO A REALITY.
ABRAMS THE PUBLISHER
MAGGIE THE EDITOR
CHAD THE ART DIRECTOR
JUSTIN THE AGENT
AND THESE LITTLE GUYS: OUR VERY SPECIAL *RESEARCH LAB*--THE WORLD'S FIRST HISTORY DEPARTMENT STAFFED ENTIRELY BY **ADORABLE BABIES!**
HEY, BABIES!
SSSSSSHH! WE ARE TRYING TO RESEARCH H.H.H. BOOK TWO!
HISTORY OF THE CIVI
OOH! WHAT'S BOOK TWO ABOUT?
CIVIL WAR IRONCLADS
CIVIL WAR
NEAT!
LOOK AT THEM! AREN'T THEY CUTE?
SSSSSHH!
BABIES, CAN YOU TELL US A LITTLE ABOUT YOUR RESEARCH FOR **ONE DEAD SPY**?
WHAP
YEAH, OKAY.
WOW! YOU BABIES READ ALL OF THESE BOOKS?
BIBLIOGRAPHY STACKS AUTHORIZED BABIES ONLY!
WASHINGTON'S SPIES ALEXANDER ROSE 2006
1776 DAVID McCULLOUGH 2005
NATHAN HALE: PATRIOT SPY SHANNON ZEMLICKA, SHANNON KNUDSEN CRAIG ORBACK 2002
AMERICAN REVOLUTION (DK EYEWITNESS BOOKS) STUART MURRAY 2005
INVISIBLE INK: SPYCRAFT OF THE AMERICAN REVOLUTION JOHN A. NAGY 2009
AS IF AN ENEMY'S COUNTRY RICHARD ARCHER 2010
THE BOSTON MASSACRE DEE READY · 2002
HENRY KNOX VISIONARY GENERAL OF THE AMERICAN REVOLUTION MARK PULS 2008
HENRY KNOX: BOOKSELLER, SOLDIER, PATRI ANITA SILVEY 2010
THE FOUNDING OF THE UNITED STATES EXPERIENCE 1763-1815 GERRY AND JANET SOUTER 2006
GEORGE WASHINGTON SPYMASTER: HOW THE AMERICANS OUTSPIED THE BRITISH AND WON THE WAR-THOMAS B. ALLEN 200
NATHAN HALE M. WILLIAM PHELPS 2008
BY THE SWORD - SELENE CASTROVILLA 2
ORIGINS OF THE AMERICAN REVOLUTION JOHN C. MILLER 1943
NATHAN HALE: REVOLUTIONARY HERO LOREE LOUGH 2000
DON'T KNOW MUCH ABOUT HISTORY KENNETH C. DAVIS 1990
WE RESEARCHED ALL THESE BOOKS TO MAKE SURE THE STORY OF NATHAN HALE WAS AS HISTORICALLY CORRECT AS POSSIBLE.

THESE BOOKS ARE ALL SECONDARY SOURCES. DIDN'T YOU USE ANY *ACTUAL* RESEARCH DOCUMENTS, LIKE NEWSPAPERS AND JOURNALS FROM THE PERIOD?

NO. THE PEOPLE AT THE LIBRARY WON'T GIVE US THAT STUFF.

WHY NOT?

BECAUSE WE'RE **BABIES!**

OH, RIGHT. YOU NEED A COLLEGE DEGREE TO GET INTO THE ORIGINAL DOCUMENTS. DO YOU HAVE ONE?

I DID A YEAR OF ART SCHOOL.

WOW.

I'M SURE THE JOB OFFERS JUST **POUR IN.**

YOU ARE A MEAN BABY.

HEY! DO WE INTERRUPT WHEN **YOU** ARE TRYING TO **DRAW?**

WE'VE GOT BOOKS TO **RESEARCH!**

NATHAN HALE'S HAZARDOUS TALES, RESEARCHED BY BABIES SINCE 2010.

HIT THE ROAD.

OUR BABIES DO EXCELLENT RESEARCH, I'VE HEARD IT IS ALMOST 76% ACCURATE.

WHEN WE **DO** GET SOMETHING WRONG IN THE BOOK, OUR **CORRECTION BABY** SEES THAT IT GETS FIXED.

CORRECTION BABY

DEAR CORRECTION BABY, I LIKE THE SCENE WHERE GENERAL WASHINGTON READS THE DECLARATION OF INDEPENDENCE TO THE TROOPS, ON PAGES 64-65. BUT ACCORDING TO MANY ACCOUNTS, IT DIDN'T HAPPEN THAT WAY. WASHINGTON HAD HIS OFFICERS READ IT OUT TO SMALLER GROUPS.

C.B. We use artistic license for that scene. Nice sunset, huh? Maybe Washington read it like that once. He was there. Why not?

DEAR CORRECTION BABY, NICE HAIRCUT. THERE IS NO EVIDENCE THAT NATHAN HALE TOOK PART IN BUILDING THE FORT ON THE DORCHESTER HEIGHTS.

C.B. He was there. Do you think he just watched everybody else work? No way. Nathan Hale helped out. He was a helper.

DEAR CUTE LI'L CORRECTION BABY, WERE NATHAN HALE AND HENRY KNOX (THE OX) *REALLY* FRIENDS?

C.B. They were in the same places at the same time. Why not be friends?

DEAR CORRECTION BABY, HOW DID HENRY KNOX GET THAT CANNON OUT OF THE FROZEN RIVER?

C.B. Don't really know. Sources just say it fell in and he got it out.

DEAR C.B. THIS ISN'T A CORRECTION, JUST A QUESTION. HOW EXACTLY DID HENRY KNOX LOSE THOSE FINGERS?

C.B. Shotgun. Never play with shotgun. ♡ *correction baby*

HAVE A CORRECTION OR QUESTION ABOUT HALE'S HAZARDOUS HISTORY? SEND IT TO: CORRECTIONBABY@HAZARDOUSTALES.COM

AM I IN TIME TO TELL MY STORY?

CRISPUS ATTUCKS!

YOU ARE JUST IN TIME!

YOU SURE? I DON'T WANT TO CROWD OUT YOUR STORY.

I'M SURE. MY LIFE STORY IS OVER.

THANKS, NATE, I'VE BEEN WANTING TO TELL MY TALE.

ANYTHING FOR MY BROTHER.

YOU GUYS ARE BROTHERS?

WE'RE IN THE BROTHERHOOD OF AMERICAN MARTYRS

B.A.M.

WHAT'S A MARTYR?

NOTHING. WHAT'S A MARTYR WITH YOU?

HA·HA·HA! HEE·HEE! HOO.

THAT JOKE NEVER GETS OLD.

A MARTYR IS SOMEONE WHO SACRIFICES SOMETHING FOR A CAUSE OR PRINCIPLE.

IN OUR CASE, THE CAUSE WAS AMERICAN INDEPENDENCE, THE SACRIFICE WAS OUR LIVES.

THAT'S CRAZY.

I NEVER WANT TO BE A MARTYR!

I DON'T BLAME YOU. I DIED FOR FREEDOM, BUT I NEVER GOT TO REALLY BE FREE.

AND THE SAD THING IS, MY PEOPLE WON'T TRULY BE FREE FOR ANOTHER CENTURY OR SO.

A *HALE'S HAZARDOUS* HISTORY MINI·COMIC

CRISPUS ATTUCKS
First to Defy, First to Die!

WOW! THIS LOOKS SERIOUS!

GET IT?

YOU COULD SAY IT'S A MARTYR OF LIFE AND DEATH!

THAT AIN'T FUNNY, HANGMAN.

UH·UH.

ONLY MARTYRS ARE ALLOWED TO MAKE MARTYR JOKES.

SORRY...

...I DIDN'T KNOW.

I WAS BORN IN SLAVE COUNTRY.

I ALWAYS WANTED TO BE FREE.

MY FATHER WAS A SLAVE.

MY MOTHER WAS FROM THE WAMPANOAG TRIBE.

I WAS A BIG KID.

SO MY FATHER'S MASTER SOLD ME.

I RAN AWAY.

I WENT NORTH.

I JOINED UP ON A WHALING SHIP.

I WAS A GOOD WHALER TOO.

I COULD HARPOON WITH THE BEST OF THEM.

WHEN I WASN'T ON A SHIP, I WORKED ON THE DOCKS.

I WAS STRONG. I COULD CARRY MORE THAN MOST.

IT WAS HARD WORK, BUT I GOT *PAID*, SO IT WASN'T *SLAVE* WORK.

I WAS WORKING IN BOSTON WHEN THE SOLDIERS CAME.

THIS WAS BACK IN 1765, BEFORE THE WAR.

WHERE'S THE WAR, BOYOS?

RIGHT HERE IF YOU CAUSE ANY TROUBLE.

BEFORE WE KNEW IT, THE SOLDIERS BEGAN TAKING OUR JOBS AT THE DOCK.

HEY! WE UNLOAD THE SHIPS!

WE DO NOW.

STEP ASIDE, YOU *RABBLE*! LET THESE GOOD ENGLISHMEN DO THEIR WORK!

NOBODY LIKED THE SOLDIERS.

121

NOT THE SHOPKEEPERS...

ARE YOU SELLING SMUGGLED GOODS?!

...NOT THE TOWNSPEOPLE...

UNDER THE *TREASON ACT* OF 1543, I COULD ARREST YOU AND SEND YOU OFF TO *ENGLAND!*

SEND YOUR-SELF OFF TO ENGLAND.

...NOT THE SAILORS. WE HAD TO *HIDE* FROM PRESS GANGS WHO WOULD FORCE US INTO SERVICE ON BRITISH SHIPS.

YER IN THE NAVY NOW!

NOBODY WANTED THE RED-COATS IN BOSTON. BUT KING GEORGE JUST KEPT SENDING THEM.

IN 1768, ONE OUT OF EVERY TEN PEOPLE IN BOSTON WAS A REDCOAT!

BY 1770, WE WERE SICK OF IT!

YOU WERE SICK OF IT? *WE* WERE SICK OF IT!

LET HIM TELL THE STORY!!

HE'S RIGHT. THE SOLDIERS DIDN'T WANT TO BE THERE EITHER.

WE HATED BOSTON.

IN 1770, TWO REGIMENTS SHIPPED OUT TO HALIFAX, LEAVING *HALF* AS MANY SOLDIERS.

THE ONES WHO STAYED IN BOSTON WERE--

LONELY?

SAD?

--PICKED ON! HARASSED! ANNOYED! *ASSAULTED!*

KNOCKED DOWN IN THE STREET BY COMMON *SCOUNDRELS!*

DID THEY FIGHT BACK?

NO, SIR, THEY DID *NOT.* UNTIL--

--UNTIL *MARCH* OF 1770.

EVERYONE WAS READY FOR A *BRAWL.*

BOSTON WAS PRIMED TO *EXPLODE.*

122

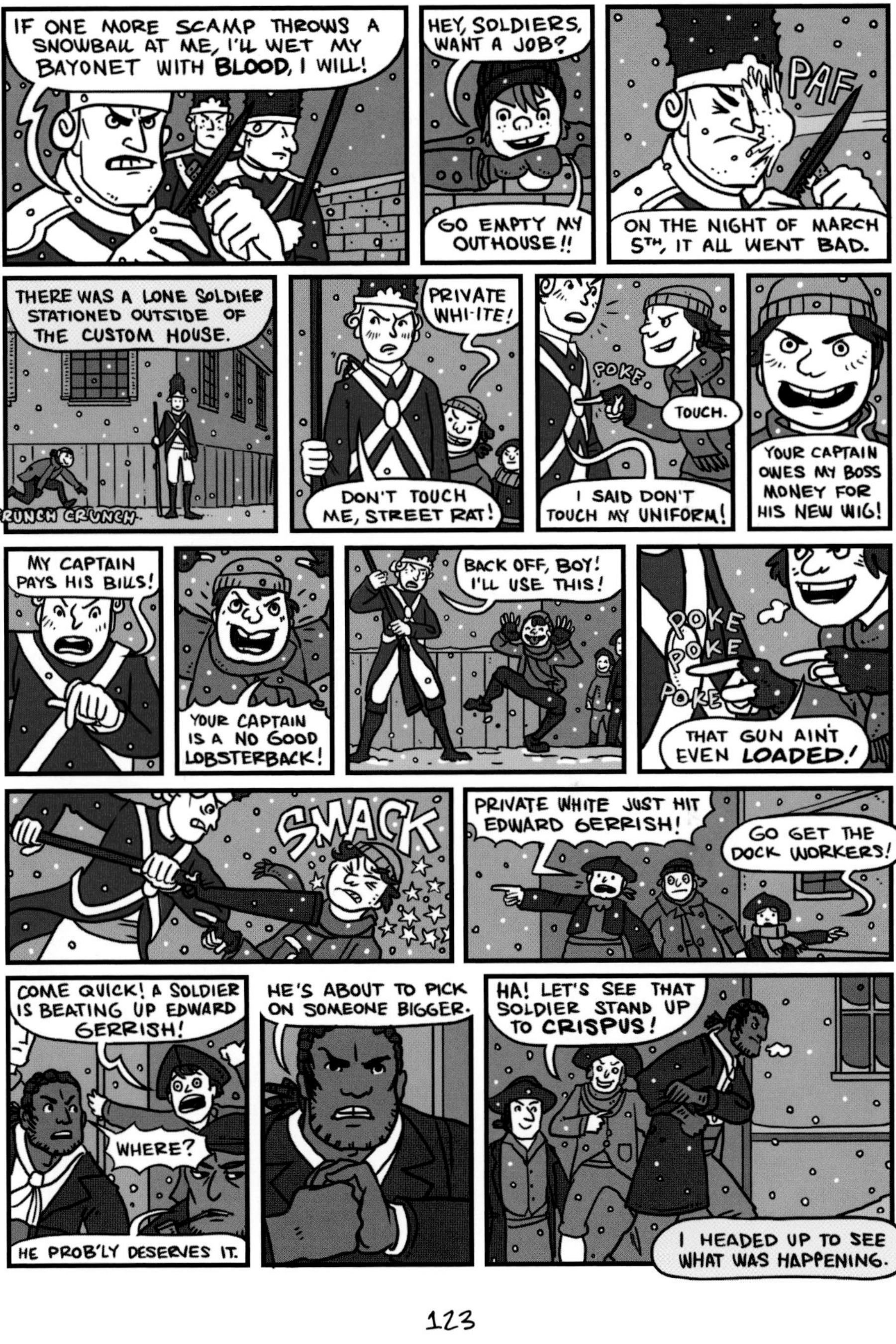
IF ONE MORE SCAMP THROWS A SNOWBALL AT ME, I'LL WET MY BAYONET WITH BLOOD, I WILL!
HEY, SOLDIERS, WANT A JOB?
GO EMPTY MY OUTHOUSE!!
PAF
ON THE NIGHT OF MARCH 5TH, IT ALL WENT BAD.
THERE WAS A LONE SOLDIER STATIONED OUTSIDE OF THE CUSTOM HOUSE.
CRUNCH CRUNCH
PRIVATE WHI-ITE!
DON'T TOUCH ME, STREET RAT!
POKE
TOUCH.
I SAID DON'T TOUCH MY UNIFORM!
YOUR CAPTAIN OWES MY BOSS MONEY FOR HIS NEW WIG!
MY CAPTAIN PAYS HIS BILLS!
YOUR CAPTAIN IS A NO GOOD LOBSTERBACK!
BACK OFF, BOY! I'LL USE THIS!
POKE POKE POKE
THAT GUN AIN'T EVEN LOADED!
SMACK
PRIVATE WHITE JUST HIT EDWARD GERRISH!
GO GET THE DOCK WORKERS!
COME QUICK! A SOLDIER IS BEATING UP EDWARD GERRISH!
WHERE?
HE PROB'LY DESERVES IT.
HE'S ABOUT TO PICK ON SOMEONE BIGGER.
HA! LET'S SEE THAT SOLDIER STAND UP TO CRISPUS!
I HEADED UP TO SEE WHAT WAS HAPPENING.

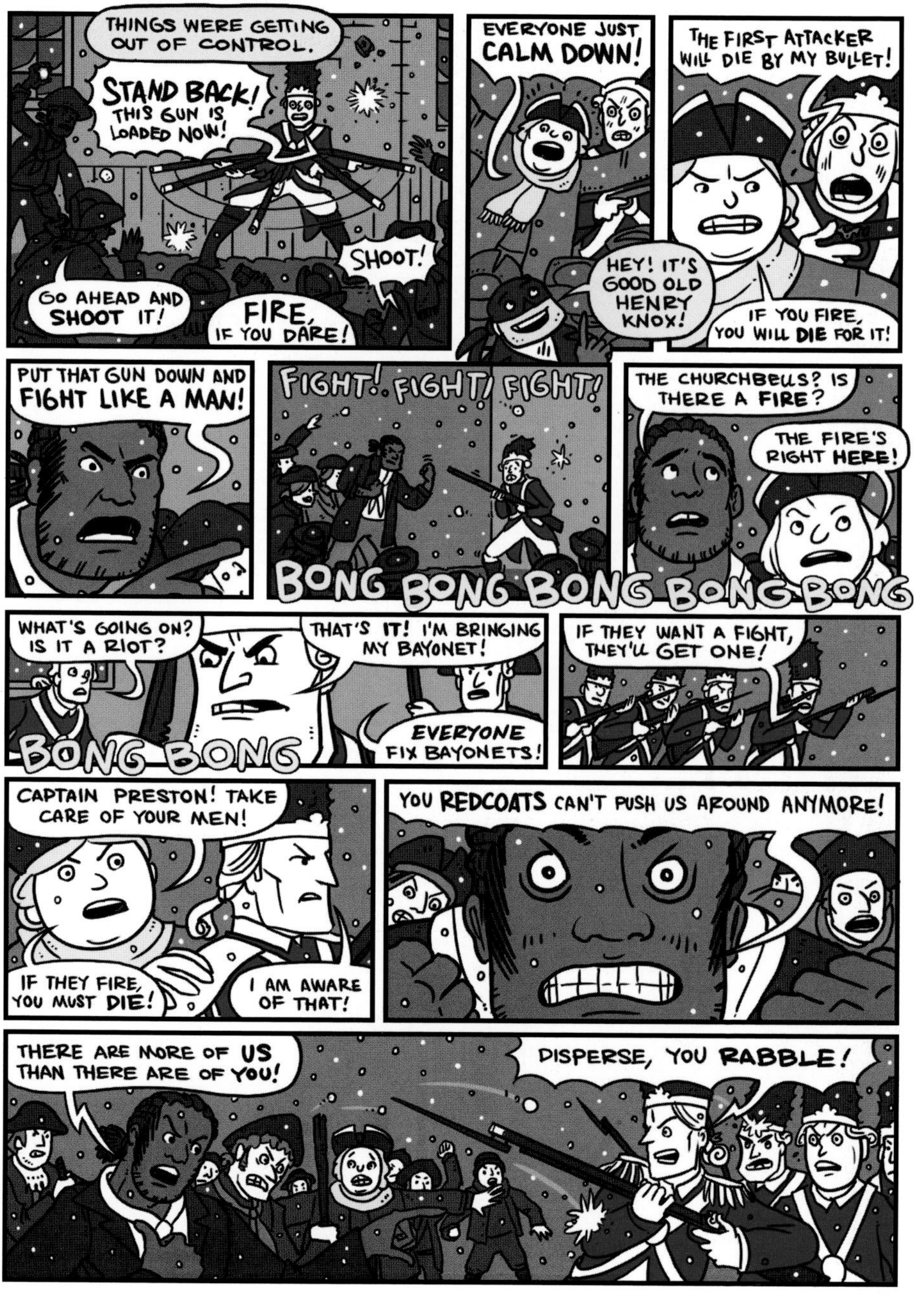
THINGS WERE GETTING OUT OF CONTROL.
STAND BACK! THIS GUN IS LOADED NOW!
GO AHEAD AND SHOOT IT!
FIRE, IF YOU DARE!
SHOOT!
EVERYONE JUST CALM DOWN!
HEY! IT'S GOOD OLD HENRY KNOX!
THE FIRST ATTACKER WILL DIE BY MY BULLET!
IF YOU FIRE, YOU WILL DIE FOR IT!
PUT THAT GUN DOWN AND FIGHT LIKE A MAN!
FIGHT! FIGHT! FIGHT!
BONG BONG BONG BONG BONG
THE CHURCHBELLS? IS THERE A FIRE?
THE FIRE'S RIGHT HERE!
WHAT'S GOING ON? IS IT A RIOT?
BONG BONG
THAT'S IT! I'M BRINGING MY BAYONET!
EVERYONE FIX BAYONETS!
IF THEY WANT A FIGHT, THEY'LL GET ONE!
CAPTAIN PRESTON! TAKE CARE OF YOUR MEN!
IF THEY FIRE, YOU MUST DIE!
I AM AWARE OF THAT!
YOU REDCOATS CAN'T PUSH US AROUND ANYMORE!
THERE ARE MORE OF US THAN THERE ARE OF YOU!
DISPERSE, YOU RABBLE!

POW POW POW POW POW POW

THAT WAS IT. THE FIRST SHOT HIT ME SQUARE IN THE CHEST.

THE CROWD BROKE. THREE OF US WERE DEAD, TWO DIED LATER.

JOHN ADAMS SAID, "ON THAT NIGHT, THE FOUNDATION OF AMERICAN INDEPENDENCE WAS LAID."

WHAT HAPPENED TO THE SOLDIERS?

THEY WERE PUT ON TRIAL. TWO WERE FOUND GUILTY OF MANSLAUGHTER.

 THEY WERE **NOT** GUILTY! THEY FIRED IN SELF-DEFENSE!

JOHN ADAMS DEFENDED THEM AT THE TRIAL.

 OOH! DID THEY HANG THEM?

 THE TWO CHARGED WITH MANSLAUGHTER HAD THEIR THUMBS BRANDED.

 OUCH! THAT MUST **HURT!**

THINK **THAT** HURTS? TRY BEING **SHOT POINT-BLANK** IN THE CHEST.

THE FIVE OF US WHO DIED WERE:

CA	SG	JC	SM	Pc

CRISPUS ATTUCKS

SAMUEL GRAY

JAMES CALDWELL

SAMUEL MAVERICK

PATRICK CARR

FOR THE NEXT FEW YEARS, THE **BOSTON MASSACRE,** AS IT WAS CALLED, WAS USED TO ANGER THE AMERICANS AGAINST BRITISH SOLDIERS.

 PAUL REVERE DREW A PICTURE SHOWING HOW HE THOUGHT THE MASSACRE HAPPENED. HE MADE PRINTS THAT WERE USED AS **ANTI-BRITISH PROPAGANDA.**

BANG! BANG!

WHAT IS POPPAGRANDO?

 PROPAGANDA IS INFORMATION PEOPLE SPREAD TO HELP, OR SOMETIMES **HARM,** SOMETHING.

HEY, LOOK, IT'S YOU!

IN THE PICTURE, THE BOSTONIANS ARE PEACE-FUL, AND THE CAPTAIN IS RAISING HIS ARM IN THE **FIRE** POSITION. THAT ISN'T HOW IT HAPPENED.

 OF **COURSE** IT ISN'T! HOW I HATE THAT PICTURE!

EVERY PATRIOT IN AMERICA HAS A COPY OF THAT PRINT.

 IT'S A COMPLETE **FABRICATION** -- CREATED TO MAKE US LOOK LIKE **VILLAINS!**

PICTURES ARE POWERFUL PROPAGANDA.

 HOLD UP. **WE** ARE PICTURES...

...ARE **WE** PROPAGANDA?

 I'M AFRAID WE MIGHT BE.

PROPAGANDA FOR LEARNING AMERICAN **HISTORY.**

126

I DON'T WANT TO BE AMERICAN PROPAGANDA!

I DIDN'T WANT TO BE PROPAGANDA OR A MARTYR.

YOU DIDN'T?

OF COURSE NOT! I WENT OUT THAT NIGHT TO FIGHT! I WANTED TO PUNCH A FEW BULLIES IN THE FACE! I WANTED TO STRIKE OUT AT THOSE WHO WANTED TO CONTROL ME!

I WAS TIRED OF BEING PUSHED AROUND BY SOLDIERS--BY SLAVE OWNERS--I WANTED TO BE FREE! SO I FOUGHT!

AFTER MY DEATH, THEY NAMED ME A MARTYR FOR AMERICAN INDEPENDENCE, BUT I DIDN'T DIE FIGHTING FOR A COUNTRY!

I DIED FIGHTING FOR FREEDOM!

AND THAT IS MY STORY.

NICELY DONE, CRISPUS!

SURE THING, BROTHER. SAY, HOW DID YOU GET THIS JOB TELLING U.S. HISTORY?

I'M IN THE HISTORY BOOK TOO.

JUST LUCKY, I GUESS.

THAT'S OKAY, I'VE GOT PLANS FOR A BOOK SERIES OF MY OWN.

ATTUCKS ATTACKS THE ATLAS

HEY, GOOD LUCK WITH THAT. AND THANKS FOR STOPPING BY.

GOODBYE, CHRISTMAS ATTICS.

SURE THING. I'LL SEE YOU AT THE NEXT MARTYRS' MEETING.

POOF

WHERE'D HE GO? WAS HE A... G-G-G-GHOST?

OF COURSE. HE DIED AT THE END OF HIS STORY, REMEMBER?

YES. B-BUT WAIT... ARE YOU A G-G-G-GHOST?

DID YOU HANG ME YET?

NO.

THEN I'M NOT A GHOST.

PHEW. THAT'S LUCKY.

YOU'RE TELLING ME...

THE SPY NATHAN HALE
WAS EXECUTED IN 1776.

THE *AUTHOR* NATHAN HALE
WAS BORN IN 1976.

NATHAN IS THE ILLUSTRATOR OF THE EISNER-NOMINATED
RAPUNZEL'S REVENGE AND ITS SEQUEL, CALAMITY JACK.
HE HAS WRITTEN AND ILLUSTRATED SEVERAL BOOKS,
INCLUDING THE DEVIL YOU KNOW, THE TWELVE BOTS OF
CHRISTMAS, AND YELLOWBELLY AND PLUM GO TO SCHOOL.

NATHAN LIVES IN THE MOUNTAINS OF UTAH WITH HIS
WIFE AND TWO CHILDREN. HE POSTS WEEKDAY
COMICS ON HIS WEBSITE:
WWW.SPACESTATIONNATHAN.COM

THANKS:
BARRY DEUTSCH, JAKE RICHMOND,
AND MATTHEW HOLM (OF *HEREVILLE*
AND *BABYMOUSE,* RESPECTIVELY) FOR ADVICE
AND TIPS ON SPOT-COLOR ILLUSTRATION.

SPECIAL THANKS:
MAGGIE AND CHAD FOR TAKING
THE RAW IDEA OF THIS SERIES AND
MOLDING IT INTO THIS RAD FINAL PRODUCT.
AND JUSTIN AT SHANNON ASSOCIATES FOR
PLACING THIS PROJECT AT AMULET.

VERY SPECIAL THANKS:
MINDY, ULYSSES, AND LUCY!

2012

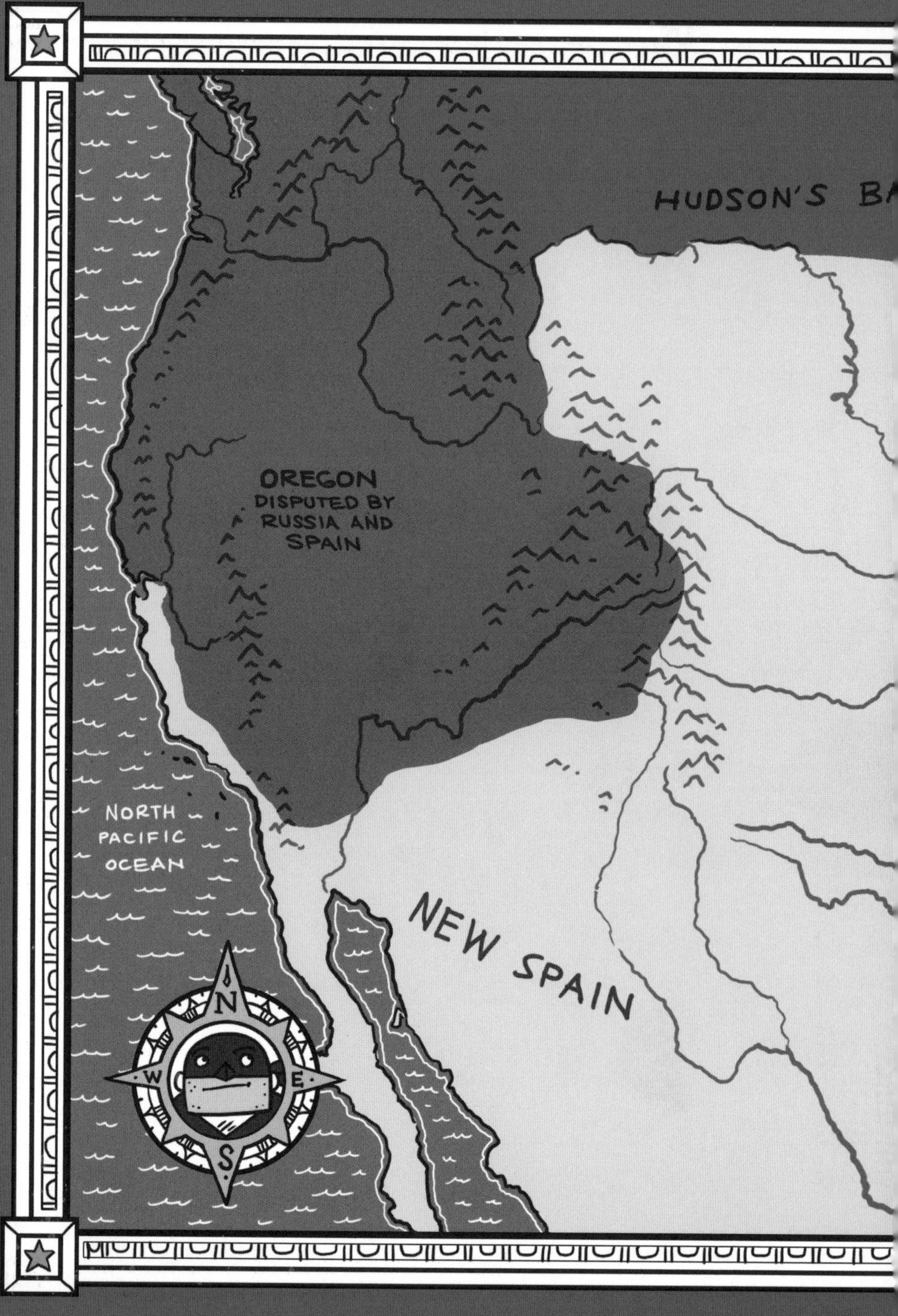
HUDSON'S
OREGON
DISPUTED BY RUSSIA AND SPAIN
NORTH PACIFIC OCEAN
NEW SPAIN
N
W
E
S